TNR Past Present *and* Future

TNR Past Present *and* Future

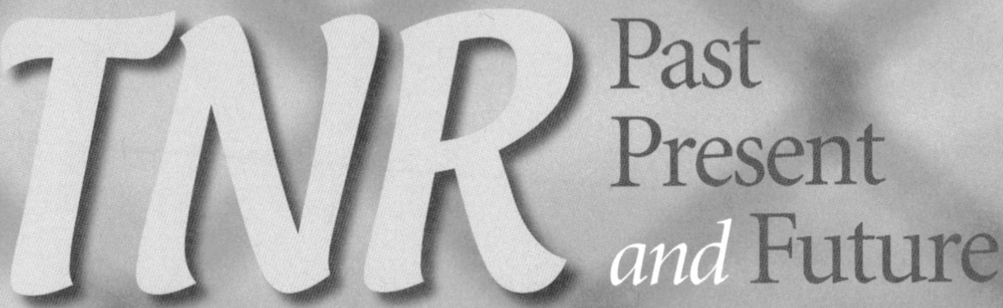

A HISTORY OF THE **TRAP-NEUTER-RETURN** MOVEMENT

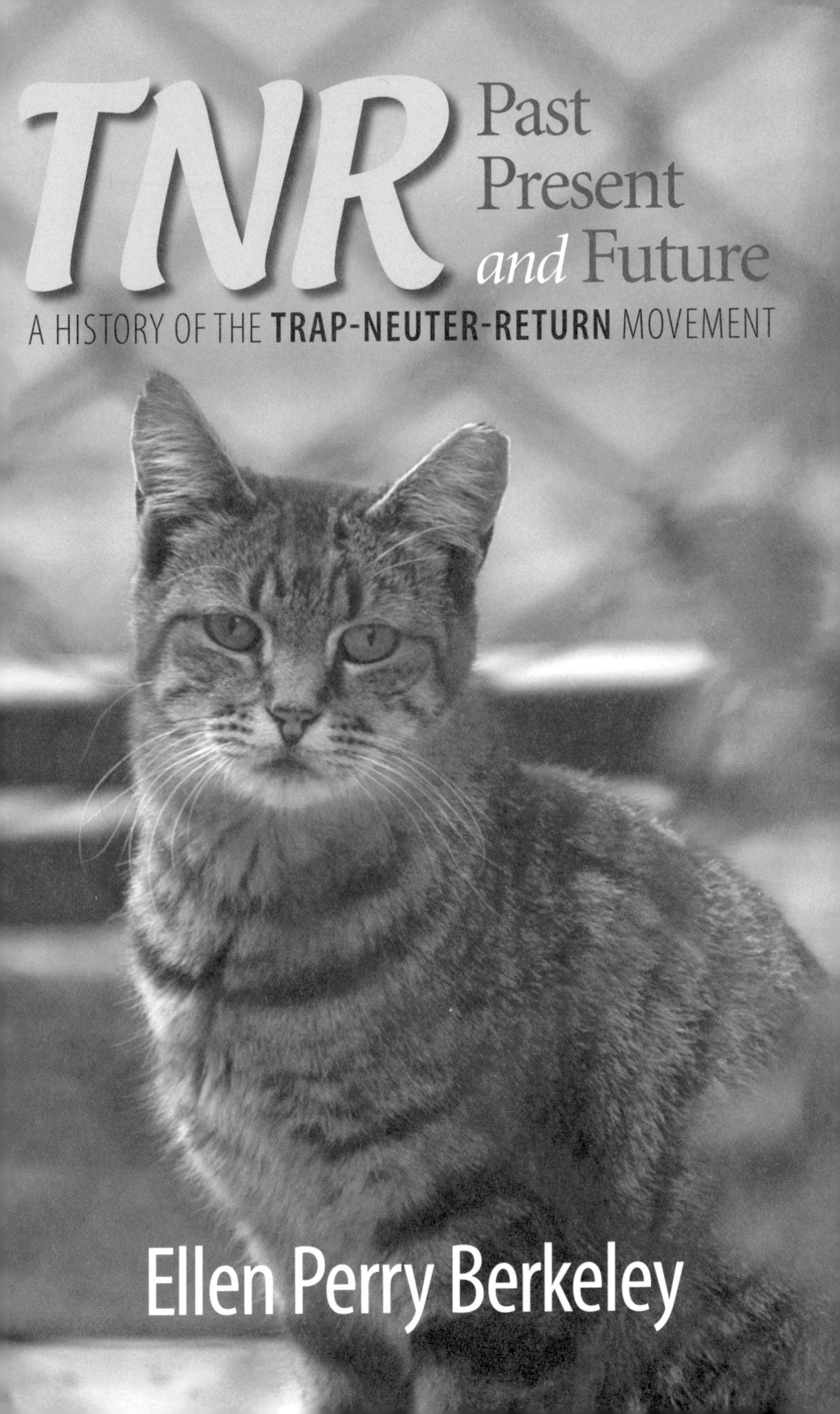

Ellen Perry Berkeley

Alley Cat Allies
1801 Belmont Road NW, Suite 201
Washington, DC 20009-5147

For additional copies of this book, please write Alley Cat Allies or visit our website at www.alleycat.org.

Photo credits and copyright: George Brinkman, Kaye S. Counce, Richard Counce, Tom Delaney, Marianne Desapio, John Newton, Troy Snow, Meredith Weiss, Susan Woodhouse

Publisher's Cataloging-In-Publication Data

Berkeley, Ellen Perry.
TNR past present and future: a history of the trap-neuter-return movement / Ellen Perry Berkeley.

p.: ill. ; cm.
Includes index.
ISBN: 0-9705194-2-7

1. Feral cats. 2. Feral cats—Control. 3. Animal contraception. 4. Animal welfare. 5. Animals—Treatment. I. Title.

SF450 .B37 2004
636.8

2004112436

Contents

Author's Note

As the TNR movement has grown, an accessible written history of the movement has seemed ever more necessary—to support the efforts of TNR advocates, to expose the misunderstandings and falsehoods of TNR detractors, and, ultimately, to give a better life to the many feral cats still to be trapped, neutered, returned, and managed/ monitored by loving caretakers.

My work on this history began in the last century, when Louise Holton (cofounder of Alley Cat Allies), was thinking of a handbook for people thinking of doing TNR. The history you see here is much longer than a chapter in a handbook—longer because there is more to discuss (only now could there be sections on nonsurgical sterilization and on recent research, for instance), longer too because the spurious arguments of a well-funded opposition must be refuted in detail for use by all who care about the cats.

I am indebted to many people who have helped to make this written history a reality. I certainly thank all who answered my requests for information. Listing them here would mean repeating all the names that appear in the Notes. (Incidentally, these Notes do more than cite a published work or date a conversation. In the Notes, I have often included additional material that would have been intrusive or "off on a tangent" if in the text.)

I am exceedingly grateful to Alley Cat Allies—Becky Robinson, national director, in particular—for ACA's eagerness to publish this history of mine, even after the written history became far too long to be considered simply a "factsheet." And I especially thank Kris Rerecich, publications director of ACA, who saw the project through its recent drafts with a patience and a pleasure that I have appreciated enormously.

Finally, of course, I thank all the feral cats—those close to me, and those close to many others—who have taught me and brought me so much. It is for the cats, ultimately, that we need a history of TNR. The growth of this movement has already changed so many cats' lives for the better. As we realize the accomplishments of TNR, we can only be spurred to do more.

—Ellen Perry Berkeley

CHAPTER ONE
Off and Running in England

TNR, of course, stands for "Trap-Neuter-Return." For fifty years and under various names, the TNR method of controlling feral cat numbers has been performed by a growing body of advocates who know TNR to be the most caring, most economical, and most effective method yet known. The following pages will detail this TNR movement—how it began, why it has grown, and where it stands now.

First, its name. Not long ago, the initials TNR stood for "trap-neuter-release." Somewhat earlier, the pioneering British used the label "neuter-and-release," while the pioneering Danish used the terms "reintroduction scheme" and "reintroduction of neutered cats." The current label in Australia is "sterilize and return to home." In other words, we've had quite a few words for this procedure. Today, in the United States, some people call it TTVAR-M or TTVARM for trap-test-vaccinate-alter-release-maintain, although even these people must occasionally make a serious effort, as I have just done, to remember what all the letters stand for. (Indeed, I've increasingly seen the "R" used for "return" instead of "release"; the "M" used for "manage" or "monitor" instead of "maintain." And some people drop the "M" altogether, yielding TTVAR.) I've also seen TNRM and TTVNR, but let's stop here. By whatever name, the practice has had a substantial history. It also has a vibrant present and an assured future. I'll call it simply TNR in the following pages.

Celia Hammond retreats to "neutering and returning to site"

Despite the occasional people who think they invented TNR themselves, the practice goes back at least to the 1950s. Several people are known to have been doing it in England at that time.[1] But it wasn't until the 1960s there, that former model Celia Hammond began getting good publicity for her "neutering and returning to site" of feral cats. She came to this work reluctantly, realizing that trapping, taming, and re-homing—her earlier effort—had proven, in her words, "hopelessly inefficient."[2]

By 1970, Hammond was keeping detailed records of neutered colonies.[3] Ten years later, she could document the considerable advantages of this method of control: it was cheaper, more efficient, more humane, and—not least—more acceptable to the public.[4] From her observations of "many hundreds of neutered colonies," she could report in 1980 that neutering had stabilized the colonies "without any detrimental effect whatsoever."[5]

British efforts owe much to the work of Celia Hammond. She was chosen first chairman of the National Cat Rescue Co-ordinating Committee (NCRCC), a British group founded in 1975 by animal activist Ruth Plant. Here was another woman ahead of her time. Ruth Plant believed firmly—heretically, in those days—that animal welfare work shouldn't be limited to pets but should also serve stray and feral animals.[6] (Late in her life, though, Plant told me that Celia Hammond was the "real hero" of the early efforts for feral cats, launching into popular awareness both the idea and the method of neutering colonies.[7])

The various animal welfare organizations represented in the British NCRCC, coming from a variety of viewpoints, soon found themselves unable to unite behind a cohesive and aggressive plan for the cats. Recognizing the impasse, two members of the group—Marilda Carey of the Royal Society for the Prevention of Cruelty to Animals, and Nerea de Clifford of the Cats Protection League—created a wholly new organization, the Cat Action Trust (CAT).[8] This effort was aided by veterinarian Dr. Jenny Remfry who had joined NCRCC as technical adviser in 1976. Officially chartered as a national charity in 1977, the pioneering CAT has worked all these years solely on neutering feral cats and returning them to their sites. The organization today is divided into two groups and has more than two dozen branches of dedicated volunteers across Britain.

UFAW holds a ground-breaking symposium

Celia Hammond was one of 14 speakers at the symposium "The Ecology and Control of Feral Cats," held in London in 1980. This ground-breaking gathering was organized by the Universities Federation for Animal Welfare (UFAW), which, since its founding in 1926 as the University of London Animal Welfare Society, has helped to devise new policies combining the practical with the humane for a wide variety of animals—wild animals, companion animals, farm animals, zoo animals, and laboratory animals.

It is fair to say that UFAW's symposium was a defining event, a watershed occurrence. Before 1980, feral cats were largely considered vermin; after 1980, they were beginning to be considered worthy of humane treatment. Dr. Jenny Remfry, then assistant director of UFAW, deserves enormous credit for this change in attitude. But as she modestly relates it, the symposium was born when veterinarian Roger Ewbank became director of UFAW in 1979 and became interested in what Remfry was doing with feral cats; "he thought the time was ripe to put the ecologists in touch with the people advocating population control," Remfry has told me.[9]

The UFAW symposium brought together a small but concerned group involved with feral cats. The symposium had two distinct purposes, as described by UFAW: 1) to provide a platform for the recent scientific explorations on feral cats (particularly on social behavior and population dynamics as these might affect methods of control); and 2) to assess the problems caused by feral cats and the methods used to control their growing numbers.[10]

Tom Kristensen, a veterinarian representing Denmark's Society for the Protection of the Cat, spoke at the symposium about the "most satisfactory" results of the society's "reintroduction" efforts in Denmark in the mid-1970s.[11] (Interestingly, as was apparent in Kristensen's presentation, ear tattooing and eartipping were routinely done in Denmark at that time.[12] Years later, at a TNR site in Tunisia, hotel guests would wonder whether the ear-tipped cats were afflicted with some local disease![13])

Jenny Remfry spoke at the symposium about UFAW's decision to pursue the trap-and-neuter program she had seen in Denmark.[14] (By 1976 she had observed two pioneering programs for feral cats in Denmark, the other program using contraceptive drugs. And by 1977, she had also done her own contraceptive trial with UFAW.) As Remfry tells it, UFAW opted for trap-and-neuter for two reasons: because it wouldn't produce the health problems that the contraceptive trials were showing due to sporadic dosing, and because it wouldn't involve the difficulties of getting a contraceptive dose to each cat on a regular basis.[15]

At the symposium, Remfry gave statistics from 38 of the earliest neutered colonies in Greater London. The data showed that the cats could be trapped, could be returned to their original sites (or could be homed, or taken to sanctuaries or farms), and could become less wary of humans afterward.[16] Most importantly, the data showed that "trapping, neutering and returning to site enabled a colony to be maintained at a desired level."[17] In other words, it worked. So well, in fact, that to avoid having a colony gradually reduced to zero (through accidents and old age), Remfry advised leaving one female unneutered.[18]

British biologist Roger Tabor also spoke at the UFAW symposium.[19] Mentioning his study group of neutered cats in London's Fitzroy Square—a group of black-and-white cats similar in coloring to T. S. Eliot's famous "Jellicle Cats"—Tabor noted that the resident cats, "even a few years after neutering, still maintain their tight family cohesiveness and still continue to exclude other cats."[20]

I devoured every word of the UFAW symposium, published in 1981, and I passed along what I considered its most important points in my book *Maverick Cats: Encounters with Feral Cats*, published a year later (and reissued in 2001 in an expanded and updated edition).[21] I was able to note, in my book, that Britain's major humane organization—the Royal Society for the Prevention of Cruelty to Animals (RSPCA)—had given its highest recommendation to the neutering of whole colonies in 1981.[22] This recommendation by RSPCA followed a four-year study by its Working Party on Feral Cats (a working party, incidentally, that owed its creation to Celia Hammond, who was on the RSPCA Council at the time[23]). The RSPCA recommendation was tempered by only one concern: "provided that their long-term welfare is ensured."[24] But feeders, or caretakers, or cat-ladies—there are many names for them, too—have usually been plentiful and committed.

In recommending neutering-and-returning to site, RSPCA's working party considered all other methods of dealing with feral cats—leaving them alone, eradicating them completely, doing controlled culling, or administering chemical contraception—and found each of these to be less desirable than the neutering of whole colonies. One persuasive argument was that neuter-and-return was more than "a stop-gap procedure."[25] But this wasn't all. "There is indeed evidence," stated the working party's report, that when a whole colony is neutered and returned to its site, "the colony's lifestyle is manifestly improved." The colony "becomes stable, is not invaded by new arrivals, and the cats become more tractable and healthy."[26]

Things were definitely looking up for feral cats in those years.

Remfry and Neville study two colonies

Earliest research seemed especially promising. My article about the research by Jenny Remfry and Peter Neville (who had joined UFAW as her assistant) was the first extensive report on "neuter-and-release" in an American publication. This article, "Controlling Feral Cats," was the lead article in a 1984 issue of *Cat Fancy* and told of several feral cat colonies closely followed after neutering.[27] Two colonies were in Regent's Park in central London; a third was in Wandsworth, on the southwest edge of London.

For eight months at one site and twelve at the other, in Regent's Park, biologist Peter Neville made weekly observations. The major conclusions: no negative effects on the cats' health, no disruption of their social hierarchy, no immigration of new cats (until some of the neutered cats died), and no lessening of the cats' approachability by their feeders.[28] This Neville-Remfry study, in fact, showed that the neutered cats became more amicable toward each other and more friendly toward their feeder. (Years later, an 11-year study by Levy, Gale, and Gale—see Chapter 5—would report that an astounding 47 percent of the cats in feral colonies on a Florida campus could subsequently be adopted.) Primarily, of course, the Neville-Remfry study showed that this method was effective in controlling the size of these cat colonies.

A contemporaneous publication from UFAW mentioned an additional benefit from the Regent's Park control scheme: "The Park authorities are very satisfied with the scheme which has prevented the birth of any kittens for more than 18 months. They are also pleased that control has been achieved without incurring the public displeasure often encountered during schemes based on extermination."[29] Thus, this method that Neville and Remfry proclaimed "very satisfactory" for the cats—in its humaneness and its effectiveness—was also seen to appeal to an unusual coalition of humans: cat-lovers, cat-haters, and taxpayers. The cat-lovers were happy that the cats weren't multiplying and being rounded up to be killed (or becoming ill and dying, as many feral kittens do); the cat-haters were happy that the cats weren't multiplying and causing a nuisance; and the taxpayers were happy that the cats weren't multiplying and requiring a never-ending outlay of public monies for control. It is indeed an unusual coalition. Only TNR could bring these groups together!

The third study carried out by Neville and UFAW—done two years later, in 1983, at a high-rise urban housing project in Wandsworth—compared the costs of neutering with the costs of other methods of control. Results projected over a 10-year period were again highly favorable for neutering.[30]

During my visit to the Wandsworth site in 1983, Neville told me that he knew of similar neutering programs not only in Denmark but also in France, Israel, Italy, and South Africa; by 1982–84, he himself was active in establishing official programs in Tunisia, Greece, and Kenya.[31] And in his view, "lots of individuals" (on a less-than-official basis) were doing TNR "all over the world" in the 1970s.[32]

Jenny Remfry's contribution to the humane control of feral cat populations is no less than monumental. She recalls being invited to lecture for the people doing pest control in National Health Service hospitals. At first they had her on "as a comedy spot," she says, because they were so amused by the idea of "putting cats on the Pill." But when she got into neutering-and-returning-to-site, her students began taking her seriously, and within a few years the new method was widespread at psychiatric and other long-stay hospitals.[33] Later, with the help of Peter Neville, she wrote *Feral Cats: Suggestions for Control*, published by UFAW in 1982. This booklet became UFAW's best seller; an enlarged third edition, published in 1995, is still going strong. During Remfry's tenure, UFAW helped to set up many control schemes in England and overseas. UFAW's annual reports tell the story: by 1979–80, the idea was "gaining ground"; by 1984–85, attitudes were continuing to become "more enlightened"; by 1989, this method of control was "now in use in many parts of the world."

CHAPTER TWO
Crossing the Atlantic

In the U.S., "there's an army out there"

But things were happening here too. I was learning of numerous efforts at TNR in this country—several going back 15 and 20 years—and I began assembling material for another article in the feline press. This one, titled simply "Feral Cats," appeared in *Cat Fancy* in July 1990, again as the lead article.[34] I was able to mention active and enthusiastic proponents of "neuter-and-release" in places as diverse as Massachusetts and Idaho, New Jersey and Nevada, Pennsylvania and Colorado, and in situations as diverse as farming communities, suburban developments, urban neighborhoods, and island vacation spots. One group, in Ocean County, New Jersey, had been "at it for 20 years."

My article showed AnnaBell Washburn demonstrating a squeeze-side cage, and I told of her success in neutering feral cats, first on Martha's Vineyard with an organization she had founded a decade earlier to help place shelter animals, and later on Virgin Gorda in the British Virgin Islands with veterinary students from Tufts.

AnnaBell Washburn is a woman with drive and stamina. But never underestimate the value of being in the right place at the right time. In Boston, in 1984, she had attended a conference of the World Society for the Protection of Animals and heard Peter Neville speak about the worldwide success of neutering schemes. Vacationing at her house on Virgin Gorda in 1985, she learned that Dr. James N. Ross, Jr., chairman of the department of medicine at the Tufts veterinary school, had just visited the island and found it so beautiful he had joked to someone, "Let me know if I can ever be of assistance down here." As soon as AnnaBell Washburn returned to the States, she gave him a call, and senior veterinary students at Tufts began going to Virgin Gorda the next summer to do sterilization surgeries arranged by Washburn.

One enthusiastic proponent of TNR told me, in 1990, "There's an army of people out there neutering feral cats."[35] I quoted her in my article, asking readers to write to *Cat Fancy* if they were part of this army. The response was larger than any of us could have imagined: "tremendous," the magazine told me. There was definitely something in the air.

Alley Cat Allies is born

My article of 1990 mentioned a number of people whose names are familiar today: Bill Brothers of Animal Care Equipment and Services, a.k.a. ACES (whose Crestline, California, company was doing trapping workshops for anyone interested), Kathy Macklem of Cat Care Society (whose Lakewood, Colorado, organization was distributing an educational brochure about neuter-and-release), Donna Bishop of Alliance for Animals (whose inner-city Boston organization was providing how-to materials with its traps).

Alley Cat Allies (ACA), however, which is currently *the* national—and international—resource on feral cats, was missing from this article. The group didn't yet exist. Louise Holton and Becky Robinson were nevertheless part of the great "army out there." Using videos and other materials from UFAW, and encouraged further by $64 received from passing the hat at a friend's office party, they had worked to neuter an alley of 56 cats and two smaller colonies in the Adams-Morgan neighborhood of Washington, DC. (Years earlier, Louise Holton had done pioneering work with the Johannesburg SPCA on neuter-and-release.)

In 1990, deluged by requests for help from many others who were trying to neuter feral cats—and aware of the almost complete dearth of equipment, resources, and veterinary assistance for TNR—the two friends set out to form "a network for feral cats" to share their information. With their solid reputations in the animal-welfare movement, and with word spreading about their successful effort in Adams-Morgan, the network grew. Incidentally, the Adams-Morgan effort can still be considered successful—no kittens born there since 1991, reports Becky Robinson of Alley Cat Allies.

The need for a national network was soon apparent. Before the end of 1991, Alley Cat Allies had taken off. The premiere issue of *Alley Cat Action* had appeared, several hundred supporters had signed on, and ACA had done workshops at half a dozen conferences. Other ambitious enterprises soon followed, among them comprehensive print and video materials for interested individuals, a national workshop in 1994 (drawing participants from across the country), and assistance to new caretakers through a Feral Friends Network—a network that currently includes more than 1,400 individuals and organizations from 47 states and 12 foreign countries.[36]

Today, with more than a dozen years as North America's premier organization involved with feral cats, ACA is a force to be reckoned with, entering almost every struggle for TNR across the United States and around the world, and appearing consistently at conferences worldwide. The list of supporters currently stands at 75,000. In a recent redefinition of its goals, ACA decided to focus primarily on changing the public policies that relate to feral cats. This decision coincided with improving services to individuals through the organization's website (where all ACA publications are posted as soon as they are published); working with colleague organizations such as Pets911 and Best Friends Animal Society to make ACA materials even more widely available; and encouraging numerous feral cat advocacy groups across the country by providing them with advice and hands-on assistance. In yet another recent decision, ACA created the first annual National Feral Cat Day, which took place on October 16, 2001 (10th anniversary of ACA's incorporation). As Becky Robinson, national director of ACA, summed up the "roaring success" of that day, "feral cats have arrived!"[37]

The "fat cats" weigh in

While all of this attention to feral cats was exciting and supportive to those doing TNR, it naturally raised the fur of those not doing TNR. I'll cite only a few of the skeptical, defensive, and wrongheaded responses from the major humane organizations in those early days.

"When Tabby Leaves Home" was the cover story in a 1987 issue of *Animals* from the Massachusetts Society for the Prevention of Cruelty to Animals (MSPCA).[38] The authors were Michael J. Konecny and Barbara Sleeper—he a wildlife biologist who had just earned his doctorate after spending two years on the Galapagos Islands studying feral cats, and she a Ph.D. candidate who was completing her doctorate in animal behavior at the University of Washington. This article got a lot of things wrong about feral cats in general.[39] But the article outdid itself with this major error about TNR: "Since these cats cannot reproduce, they don't leave a vacuum for others from the outside to fill.[40] What a confusion of ideas! No, it is because the cats are *there* that they don't leave a vacuum. But the details didn't trouble these writers; they had already endorsed MSPCA's view that all feral cats should be euthanized.

The Humane Society of the United States (HSUS) chimed in too. In *Shelter Sense*, in 1992, an article by Rhonda Lucas Donald entitled "Should Feral Cats Be Euthanized?" managed to take a 1990 research study by UFAW (in favor of TNR) and turn it upside down (to oppose TNR).[41] The UFAW study, by Warner C. Passanisi and David W. Macdonald,[42] had concluded that "the 'neutering and returning' programme is now the most widely used method of feral cat control, and the consensus is that it is the most humane, cost-efficient, and effective means of population control available."[43] Passanisi and Macdonald admitted a lack of extensive evidence behind this view, but Rhonda Lucas Donald managed to misrepresent even the evidence they supplied. She concluded that TNR was inhumane, inappropriate, fallacious, and in some states "can even be considered illegal."[44] For Donald and for HSUS, euthanasia was "the best solution to the problem."[45] Her words were cited in 1995 by the police chief of Alexandria, Virginia, (and undoubtedly by others elsewhere) to oppose TNR.[46] Some prose, alas, is indeed deathless.

No less hostile to TNR was People for the Ethical Treatment of Animals (PETA). In my 1990 article for *Cat Fancy*, I mentioned PETA's Factsheet #10, "Trapping Feral Cats: The Animal Comes First," a two-pager which, from its bibliography, can be pegged to 1989 or 1990. This factsheet advised that feral cats should be trapped, sterilized, and "either adopted or, if their environment is conducive to their safe existence, released." Soon afterward, a revised factsheet (otherwise unchanged and similarly undated) spoke only of adoption or euthanasia. Oh, to have been a mouse in the wall during those (and later) discussions of TNR by PETA. Today on its website—www.peta.org—PETA speaks of its "serious concerns" about TNR. "Sadly," it continues, because of the "gruesome things that can happen to feral cats" (several of which are gratuitously shown in a companion brochure), PETA "cannot in good conscience" advocate TNR and "cannot in good conscience" oppose euthanasia for feral cats. TNR is acknowledged as a dim possibility, perhaps to allow PETA to say that its position "has never been that all feral cats should be euthanized." But as in years past, PETA's position today is all too clear.

CHAPTER THREE
Gaining Ground

But approval for TNR grows

At a 1991 workshop on feral cats convened by the Rhode Island Animal Control Association, a veterinarian slated to give the anti-TNR position turned to the audience after hearing Louise Holton speak. He wouldn't be giving the opposing viewpoint after all, he said, because he had just changed his mind 100 percent![47]

National meetings were held. A one-day workshop was convened in 1992 at Tufts University School of Veterinary Medicine, when Dr. Andrew N. Rowan, then director of the Tufts Center for Animals and Public Policy, decided that feral cats had become a "hot topic." A roundtable discussion for representatives of key animal groups was organized in 1994 by the Doris Day Animal League (DDAL), when a dialogue between pro and con seemed needed. ACA held its own event in 1994—its "Focus on Ferals" seminar—coordinating with DDAL to hold the two gatherings in Washington, DC, on consecutive days. The ACA's open seminar offered presentations from leading TNR advocates in the United States and the United Kingdom, and drew attendees from as far away as California and Canada. Rounding out these early events was a three-day scientific workshop in 1996 cosponsored by the American Humane Association (AHA) and the Cat Fanciers' Association(CFA), when AHA felt that feral cats had become "high profile." Change was in the wind.

It is interesting to read the proceedings of that AHA/CFA scientific workshop, with its many supportive comments from scientists, experts, and cat advocates.[48] The neutered cats have "lost the haunted look of fear and hunger," said one enthusiast.[49] "We have been overwhelmed by the positive response from the public," said another.[50] Feral cats are "entitled to more than the 'right' to death," said a leading advocate.[51] Various people mentioned the good condition of the neutered cats; more than 90 percent of them are "doing very well indeed," said a vet.[52] The group spelled out specific needs: more data on the impact of TNR, more public funding, less isolation of TNR caregivers. The group learned of San Diego's amazing 40 percent drop in euthanasia rates, a drop that occurred only two years after the Feral Cat Coalition began its TNR program there in 1992.[53] Some attendees, of course, were convinced that euthanasia of all feral cats was still the only way to go. But when people gather to exchange opinions, opinions can change.

The organizations themselves had begun to change their opinions. A further article in MSPCA's *Animals*, in 1995, continued to dismiss TNR as unworkable,[54] but attention was beginning to be paid to TNR by this influential organization. Carter Luke, vice-president of MSPCA's Humane Services Division, had issued a set of "guidelines for cat rescue" in 1993. "The MSPCA is not necessarily endorsing nor are we practicing neuter/release," he explained, "but we are trying to provide guidance for humane approaches using any kind of strategy."[55] He concentrated rather more on the difficulties of neuter/release than on its benefits. Still, this was progress.

Veterinarians were learning about TNR. In 1994, the publication *Animal People* surveyed 227 veterinarians (87 of them working in low-cost neutering programs) and found that 54 percent thought neuter-and-release an ethical approach; 24 percent thought it not ethical; the rest couldn't decide.[56] Nothing yet to cheer about, but interesting.

A year later, the American Veterinary Medical Association (AVMA) focused on the welfare of cats at its sixth annual Animal Welfare Forum, bringing in Dr. Jenny Remfry as one of eight speakers. Reporting on feral cats in Britain, she mentioned the study of the Regent's Park cats and a follow-up study of 17 neutering programs she had helped to start in 1979.[57] Whether she single-handedly turned the tide—I wouldn't doubt it—the executive board of AVMA ratified neuter-release guidelines in 1996.[58] This was, indeed, something to cheer about, even though the guidelines specified that caregivers should register with animal control authorities—a requirement not welcomed by caregivers, who were generally uneasy about having their names, addresses, and cat colonies known to the authorities at a time when animal control agencies were generally hostile to TNR.

Joan Miller, director-at-large of the Cat Fanciers' Association, the world's largest registry of pedigreed cats, also spoke at that AVMA Animal Welfare Forum, introducing there the "Touch Barrier" diagram that is still so valuable in explaining the range of cat behavior from feral to domesticated. CFA had been interested in TNR since the early 1990s, Miller tells me.[59] "To CFA, every cat is special," she says, explaining that CFA's respect for both pedigreed and nonpedigreed cats goes back to 1906. Then she adds, "But how can you raise the status of cats if your policy is to round up and kill all feral cats?"[60] In 1998, the Board of Directors unanimously approved Miller's "guidance statement" in favor of TTVARM. This statement opposed any "permit fees, caregiver registration, cat licensing, fines or other punitive measures" since these "tend to discourage otherwise caring individuals from coming to the aid of unowned/feral cats."[61]

Even the Humane Society of the United States, long considered one of the firmest holdouts against TNR, had by the end of 1998 admitted, somewhat grudgingly, that TTVARM "has its time and place."[62] Unfortunately, however, HSUS still used the word "release," allowing opponents to fall back on the old argument that it's really "neuter and abandonment." And the accompanying two-page "HSUS Statement on Free-Roaming Cats"[63] went so far as to insist that any TTVARM program should register all caregivers and license all cats.

The thinking in some quarters is that HSUS will have to prove itself, after its long history of not supporting TNR—and perhaps not quite understanding it. In fact, the 1998 policy statement committed what many consider a blunder in the first sentence of its discussion of TTVARM, suggesting that the ostensibly newer TTVARM programs are "more responsibly managed" than the "traditional trap, sterilize, and release programs."[64] Not so, of course. Only the names have changed. The best TNR programs have always included the testing, vaccinating, and monitoring that give TTVARM its many initials. Only recently have some of these very responsible TNR programs ceased testing for feline leukemia virus (FeLV) and feline immunodeficiency virus (FIV), finding that these diseases are no more prevalent among feral cats than among owned cats, and wishing to use limited funds to sterilize greater numbers of feral cats instead.[65] But rabies vaccinations? Almost always given in TNR programs. And monitoring/managing/maintaining? Always insisted upon by TNR advocates.

Not every organization jumped on the bandwagon during the 1990s. The

National Council on Pet Population Study and Policy (NCPPSP), founded in 1993 as a coalition of 11 of the nation's foremost animal organizations, has had a threefold mission—to gather data on companion animals, to promote responsible stewardship of these animals, and to recommend programs to reduce the number of surplus and unwanted pets. For more than a decade NCPPSP has done nothing on feral cats—perhaps, as NCPPSP says, because first it wanted to update its data on shelters, on pet owners, and on pet acquisition and relinquishment. A member of NCPPSP's Scientific Advisory Committee, however, suggested to me that "many of the founding (and financially supporting) members represent conventional shelter interests, so that also weighed in."[66] It would be 2003, a full 10 years after its founding, before NCPPSP would begin thinking about researching the population dynamics of free-roaming cats, a group that would include feral cats as an important component.[67]

The word spreads

From the 1990s on, TNR has been increasingly in the news.

The feline press has taken up the cause in various ways—reporting on the more prominent policy struggles over feral cats, sounding an approving note after a pertinent letter to the editor, and spotlighting some of the growing number of people dedicated to TNR (with *Cat Fancy* instituting a continuing series, "Unsung Heroes," on the people who care for feral and homeless cats). The word "feral" no longer needs to be explained in the cat magazines. The method "TNR" no longer needs to be defended. And when an article in the October 2001 *Cat Fancy* listed the nation's five "best kitty cities," all five could be seen as having a strong feral cat program.[68]

Then, too, as the no-kill movement has advanced in recent years, TNR has been saluted broadly in the movement's literature and at its conferences.

The publication *Animal People* has had some of the strongest messages in favor of TNR. (In fact, Editor Merritt Clifton and Publisher Kim Bartlett did one of the earliest major U.S. TNR projects—in Connecticut in 1991—handling 326 cats and issuing both encouragements and cautions about the process.[69]) In recent years, *Animal People* has frequently pointed to the growth of TNR as an important factor in lowering euthanasia rates across the country.[70] And in an editorial in 2002, the publication cited "the recent dramatic growth of no-kill shelters and sanctuaries, high-volume adoption centers, shelterless rescue groups, and neuter/return projects to assist feral cats" as representing "the beginning of the mop-up phase of the movement against pet overpopulation" (these, after the greater sterilization of pets had already reduced the euthanasia of healthy animals to a fraction of what it was).[71]

Animal People has given many assessments of the number of feral cats. Clifton believes that because of the significant growth in TNR over the past decade (even though "the maximum potential for using TNR effectively has only been half-realized"), the feral population in the United States may now be "as low as 13 million" with a summer peak of "no more than 24 million."[72] Continuing his optimistic estimates was his report in 2003 that the number of road-killed cats had "plummeted" 90 percent over the past decade, suggesting that the number of outdoor and feral cats had dropped by the same amount—to as few as 5 million—a drop indicating, to Clifton, that "all the effort and expense put into feral cat sterilization is paying off bigtime."[73]

Stories about TNR now appear in the general press and on television—sympathetic stories about the volunteers who are doing the difficult work and about the cats who are benefiting from it. I caught a *Jeopardy!* show where a young contestant told Alex Trebek that she was doing TNR and he smiled his encouragement, in no way considering her odd. And the comic strip "Farley" by Phil Frank, in the *San Francisco Chronicle*, regularly includes the outspoken Orwell T. Catt, member of a TNR colony in Golden Gate Park.

Yet a recent book-length mystery, *Cat's Claw*, showed no real understanding of TNR. When the leading character was faced with a yardful of someone else's cats—don't ask why—her only thoughts were these: "If I stop feeding them, they'll starve. If I keep filling their bowls, I'll be perpetuating the problem. If I call animal control, I'll be handing down a death sentence."[74] Only later does the woman think, about one of the feral cats, "I could have it neutered, then release it. Or maybe let it live in the extra bedroom." But she hastily dismisses both ideas, without further comment and without specific mention of TNR.[75] In the end, it turns out that a cat knew how to rescue our heroine—don't ask how—but our heroine didn't know how to rescue the cats.

Even with more extensive reportage on TNR, it isn't always completely favorable. The *New York Times* dealt with TNR in 2003 in a news story titled "Bird Lovers Hope to Keep Cats on a Very Short Leash."[76] The article opened with a description of a TNR caretaker, in words and photo. But with anti-TNR arguments appearing as early as the second, third, and fourth paragraphs—and throughout the article—this was hardly a balanced view of TNR. In fact, no detailed support for TNR found its way into the article. Instead, much bird-worry was scattered about. (A pull-out quote in large type proclaimed, "Feral cats by the millions play havoc in fragile environments," which surely stretches things, as it stands.) Apparently, though, it wasn't *Times* policy to oppose TNR. Within a month, the same newspaper carried an almost-fully supportive story of TNR being done with care and love in a New York City suburb in Westchester County. In this report, birds barely fluttered into the discussion.[77]

Different views within the same publication are not uncommon. As another example, *CatWatch: The Newsletter for Cat People* (from Cornell's College of Veterinary Medicine) carried an excellent article called "How to Help Homeless Cats" in its March 2003 issue.[78] TNR was described briefly but approvingly. However, in the very next issue of this newsletter, an article encouraging people to keep their cats indoors (not a bad idea) ended by advising readers to consult the American Bird Conservancy website for further information (not a good idea).[79]

Doing your research with the American Bird Conservancy can be either amusing or infuriating, depending on your ability to tolerate "facts" that are unproven at best and erroneous at worst.

Let us now confront the bird issue.

CHAPTER **FOUR**

Birds Flying In

An English village makes history

The opponents of TNR were never happily stretched out in the sunshine. But as TNR successes multiplied in the 1980s, an active opposition began to stretch its muscles. If I call this opposition "for the birds," you will immediately understand both who is behind it and how it stacks up as serious science. Joking aside, get ready for some serious "science stuff" in the next few pages. Some of these details are in no other popular discussion of this topic.

First came a research project by Peter B. Churcher and John H. Lawton, appearing initially in the Zoological Society of London's *Journal of Zoology* in 1987.[80] This study analyzed the prey brought home by the 77 cats in a small English village, concluding that birds (almost half of them sparrows) accounted for 35 percent of the total catch. Most of the prey items—64 percent—were small mammals such as wood mice, field voles, shrews, and the occasional rabbit. By the time a second article by Churcher and Lawton reached the magazine *Natural History*, it included an extrapolation to all of Britain for a total of "about 70 million" items of prey taken by house cats, of which "between 30 and 50 percent may be birds."[81] By simple mathematics, this became "at least twenty million birds a year" taken by Britain's house cats. An eager *Time* magazine rushed in with a one-pager it gaudily titled "Attack of the Killer Cats."[82]

Any serious student of these things could, and did, see various problems with Churcher and Lawton's projection. First, an extrapolation from limited numbers is always on shaky ground. During the study year, only 1,090 prey items were tallied for the 77 cats. One cat showed up with 95 items, while six cats brought nothing home. Which cats are the more representative? Then, too, as Roger Tabor points out, these village cats are not representative of the town cats (i.e., city cats) that populate Britain in far larger numbers; urban cats, with smaller ranges, catch far fewer items of prey.[83] Second, there's no way of determining, from this study, what *effect* the cats' predation had on the prey populations—to prey on a population is not necessarily to damage it.[84] And third, the guess that bird-kills could account for 30 to 50 percent of all kills is out of line with every previous study of this predator in this kind of environment.[85] Over and over again, cats have been proven to eat what they can easily take. On continents, for instance (as distinct from small, barren, isolated islands with large seabird populations), the prey of cats has been shown over and over again to consist of mammals far in excess of birds. Why? Because mammals are more readily available in the rich ecosystems of continents (and this would include rural English villages), and because mammals are more readily killed by cats. These are not matters of emotion, to be settled by whichever side gets more media coverage; they are matters of fact, proven many times over by researchers around the world.

Churcher himself is quoted in the newsletter *Catnip* (published by the Tufts University School of Veterinary Medicine) sounding a note of caution.[86] "I'd be very wary," says Churcher, "about extrapolating our results even for the rest of Britain, let alone America. I don't really go along with the idea of cats being a threat to wildlife." So much for Churcher and Lawton. But certain people would use the Churcher and Lawton data to fight TNR, as we shall see.

A nationwide campaign targets cats

In 1997, the American Bird Conservancy (ABC) launched its "Cats Indoors! The Campaign for Safer Birds and Cats." Sponsored jointly by the Humane Society of the United States (which was singled out for acknowledgment by ABC as its "principal partner in this endeavor"), this campaign was immediately supported by the National Audubon Society in a resolution from its Board of Directors and immediately promoted by the media who swallowed it in one gulp. Within a year, the American Humane Association had officially joined the campaign, lending its name and logo to those of ABC and HSUS on a colorful "Cats Indoors!" brochure.

At the core of the campaign was a 16-page report that included this statement: "Extensive studies of the feeding habits of domestic, free-roaming cats have been conducted over the last 50 years in Europe, North America, Australia, Africa, and on at least 22 islands. These studies show that approximately 60 to 70 percent of the wildlife killed [by cats] are small mammals, 20 to 30 percent are birds, and up to 10 percent are amphibians, reptiles, and insects."[87] What caught my eye was that "20 to 30 percent" for birds. Sounds like this figure comes from those "extensive studies," doesn't it (including the studies on those 22 islands)? But no responsible scientist would combine the results of cat-predation studies from Europe or North America, say, with the results of studies from small and barely inhabited islands having a totally different ecosystem. (Cats do, indeed, take a great many birds on those subantarctic and tropical islands. For two reasons. First, there are few, or no, other mammalian predators there, with the result that the birds—often ground-nesting and flightless birds—haven't developed behaviors allowing them to elude the newly arrived cats. Second, in these very simple ecosystems, there are few mammalian prey species that the cats might otherwise prefer.) Those islands, therefore, offer quite different diets to their feral cats from the diets enjoyed by the feral cats we see all around us in our richer ecosystems.

I wondered which studies from the ABC's list of references had gone into its "20 to 30 percent" figure. And did this figure represent an average of these studies? Or a range? Or was some more complicated mathematics involved, giving different weights to different studies? And why did ABC's references fail to include more than a dozen important studies I had mentioned in *Maverick Cats*, many of them containing reservations about a high bird-kill by cats, and several of them even finding birds—as measured either by weight or volume—at less than 6 percent of the total prey of the cats being studied?[88]

I wrote to the American Bird Conservancy. Two months later, after several follow-up requests, I still had no reply. Then the originator and coordinator of the "Cats Indoors!" campaign, Linda Winter, telephoned to say that she hadn't answered me in writing because "writing takes too much time," and that her reply must, in any case, be off-the-record. I was stunned. Was I the first to seek this information? And why would ABC be reluctant to release it? I held my ground, wanting the information and, if possible, wanting it in writing. I said that I like to have written materials on a complicated and controversial subject; I like to be sure we all agree on what we're talking about.

Surprisingly, Winter relented about being off-the-record. She mentioned, in this phone call, that the 20 to 30 percent figure came from researchers B. M. Fitzgerald, John S. Coleman, and Stanley A. Temple. I knew Fitzgerald's considerable work on cat predation, including his major piece, 23 pages long, for the definitive 1988 book, *The Domestic Cat: The Biology of Its Behaviour.*[89] Coleman and Temple had written several brief pieces, one of them a two-page flyer, on cats and wildlife predation.[90] Four months and several reminders after this phone call, I received a letter from Linda Winter, in which, in nine sentences, she reiterated these sources and added one more: Churcher and Lawton.[91]

Hang in there with me. This is just getting interesting. Coleman and Temple cite two figures for the percentage of birds in cats' diets—23 percent (which is from their own data, unpublished) and 20 to 30 percent (which they say is "consistent with other studies" and for this they cite Fitzgerald's chapter, "Diet of Domestic Cats and Their Impact on Prey Populations," from the 1988 volume edited by Turner and Bateson).[92] Some years ago I had been in contact with Fitzgerald about his work, so I wrote to him in New Zealand, asking whether his research had been correctly interpreted by ABC.

Fitzgerald provides real answers

Fitzgerald's reply to me was not unexpected, but was a shocker nevertheless. The "20 to 30 percent" figure from ABC is "not valid," he wrote.[93] (That's the polite way, I suspect, of saying it's "for the birds.") Fitzgerald had indeed given a 21 percent figure for birds in the diet of cats on continental lands, but he stresses that this figure was not the percentage of all prey eaten by the cats, but was the *percentage of occurrence* of birds in the guts or scats of the cats.

In other words, his 21 percent figure was simply the percentage of cat stomachs or feces, in various research projects, that contained birds in any amount. Many guts or scats, he explains, contain more than one category of prey, so when everything gets added up—the percentage of guts or scats containing mammals, plus the percentage containing birds, plus the percentage containing reptiles, plus the percentage containing insects—the sum "can greatly exceed 100 percent," Fitzgerald explains.

Clarifying this further, Fitzgerald says that "for birds, percentage of occurrence figures are much higher than percentage of all prey eaten...the figures for birds, as percentages of total vertebrate prey eaten, may be only one-half to one-third the percentage of occurrence figures." So this would put birds, as a portion of the diet of cats, at roughly 7 to 10.5 percent—nowhere near the "20 to 30 percent" figure unleashed on the unscientific public by ABC!

Fitzgerald is a highly experienced researcher and he wraps up this subject, in his letter to me, with these words: the percentage of occurrence figures for birds "cannot be converted directly into a figure for the percentage of birds in the total vertebrate prey eaten by cats, and so my figures have not been used correctly." As many of us suspected. So much for the "20 to 30 percent" figure from ABC. Those who promulgate this figure should probably be selling used cars, not trying to sell serious science.

Fitzgerald's research has gone further in the past few years. His most recent analysis of birds in the diet of cats is in the second edition (published in 2000) of the authoritative Turner and Bateson volume. Here, Fitzgerald looked at the *average frequencies* of birds in various studies of cat diet—grouping together the studies done on continents and separating them from the studies done on two different kinds of islands.[94] He is unaware of any other researcher looking at the data in this way, and—as we now know—ABC is only dimly aware of *his* research.

The results were something of a surprise, Fitzgerald says, in another letter to me.[95] Finding cats to be "primarily predators of small mammals" was no surprise, of course; it is "a point that I keep trying to emphasize," he writes. But he was "impressed" and surprised to find that "the average figures for the frequencies of birds were so similar for the two continental categories and for islands where seabirds were not recorded in the diet." These figures, soon appearing in his Turner and Bateson chapter, were 20.7 percent and 20.8 percent for the continental studies (Australia and Europe/North America, respectively, and 21.2 percent for the island studies where only landbirds—and no seabirds—were recorded in the diet.

What surprised him, too, he tells me, was that the frequency of birds in the diet of cats went way up on islands *with* seabirds recorded in the diet, rising to an average frequency of 60.6 percent: "it is predation on seabirds that increases the frequency of bird in the diet," he emphasizes in his communication to me.[96] Let's remember this when the bird people—who are as far from subantarctic and tropical islands as the rest of us—give us their statistics on birds in the diet of cats.

The battle continues

ABC's "20 to 30 percent" figure continues on its website. But an ABC brochure issued in 1998 (and still distributed) revised that claim somewhat, stating this: "Scientists estimate that cats kill hundreds of millions of birds each year and three times as many small mammals."[97] This three-to-one ratio of mammals to birds still considerably overestimates the importance of birds in the diet of cats. Confusing things further, ABC is talking *numbers* of prey individuals here, while most studies of cat diet are by *percentage of occurrence* of that prey. (Still other studies are by *weight* or *volume*; relatively few studies are by actual numbers of prey, making any such three-to-one ratio difficult to substantiate.)

The ABC website continues its claims along these lines with the statement that "cats are estimated to kill hundreds of millions of birds and more than a billion small mammals" a year.[98] To support these claims, ABC uses outdated estimates of the numbers of feral cats in the United States, and wrongly devised estimates of the number of feral cats per square mile (the latter from a Wisconsin study by Coleman and Temple). Both estimates were deftly refuted by Merritt Clifton in his major article on feral cats in the June 2003 *Animal People*.[99]

But in linking cats to a devastating destruction of birds, rodents, etc., and using this to argue for the complete removal of feral cats, ABC has provided us with an answer to the old question: when is a cat not a cat? Answer: when it is a goat—a scapegoat.

ABC shows little interest in the more frequently cited reasons for bird depletion, which include *destruction of bird habitat* as we vastly expand our own habitat; *degradation of bird habitat* as we infuse the air with our pesticides and pollution; and *fragmentation of bird habitat* as we chop the land into smaller and smaller chunks (bringing the negative consequences of "edge effect"—such as fire or drought—to the interior of a habitat, also causing inbreeding among a bird population, and bringing predation and nest parasitism from invading birds). Not to be overlooked, in addition, are the *head-on collisions* with our burgeoning cars, power lines, wind farms, and communication towers, as well as with the windows from which we happily look out upon our birds.

How do cats figure in this larger picture? ABC would seem to be denying even the existence of a larger picture. Worldwatch Institute, however, states that "loss or damage to species' living spaces poses by far the greatest threat to birds and biodiversity in general."[100] And Merritt Clifton cites the white-tailed deer, specifically, as "eating the birds out of house and home."[101] He also supplies carefully compiled figures for the annual loss of birds: 163 million birds killed by pet and feral cats; 100 million birds killed by collision with window glass; and (adding to existing counts the numbers that were "removed by scavengers or went unnoticed") 220 million birds killed by moving vehicles.[102]

I have a mischievous friend who notes that some birds—the ubiquitous bluejay among them—are prone to killing other birds. He's waiting for ABC to declare that all bluejays must be rounded up, either to be humanely euthanized or to be maintained indoors! He's kidding, obviously. But let's return to serious argument. We don't hear arguments from ABC that—according to the eminent cat researcher Paul Leyhausen—even when a relative absence of rodents concentrates the cats' energies on songbirds, the cats "almost always catch only old, sick or young specimens."[103] That's the best that many cats can do, and some of this culling may even help a bird population by improving the lot of the remaining birds.

Supporting Leyhausen's thesis is the recent report of two scientists in France who examined 500 spleens of birds killed in various ways—by cats, by windows, by cars. The spleens of the cat-killed birds were one-third to one-half smaller than the spleens of the birds killed accidentally. In part, this may have been because 70 percent of the birds taken by the cats were young birds, compared to 50 percent of the birds who died accidentally. But smaller spleens also indicate problems of infection and parasite infestation in birds. And thus the argument can reasonably be made, as *Cats & Kittens* editorialized about this research by Anders Moller and Johannes Erritzoe, that "by harvesting the slower moving youngsters—or the ones that fall or are pushed out of the nest—cats appear to be ensuring that only the fittest birds survive to reproduce."[104]

It seems safe to conclude that except for places in the continental United States where an unusual situation may put birds in danger of reduction to the point of extinction—one such place may be a series of canyons in the San Diego area[105]—the effect of cat predation on American birds has been seriously overstated by the American Bird Conservancy. (In contrast, Alley Cat Allies can cite locations where cats have been in place near endangered birds and mammals for many years with no negative effect on these endangered species.[106])

Why are the errors in ABC's "Cats Indoors!" campaign of importance? Because while it is often salutary to keep cats indoors—pet cats and tame cats, that is, because it isn't an option for feral cats—the aims of this campaign are subtler, and larger. The 1998 brochure urged people to support legislation requiring cats to be registered and kept from roaming; it urged people not to feed any unowned cats without trying to secure for them a permanent home indoors; and it urged people to take any cats they cannot care for to the local animal shelter for "the best possible chance of adoption."[107] This portion of the ABC brochure was under the heading "For the Sake of All Cats." But where were *feral* cats in ABC's vision? The word "feral" did not even appear in the brochure, and ABC seemed not to understand the fate awaiting the average feral cat at the average animal shelter. (On its website today, ABC does mention managed colonies, putting "managed" in quotes and quickly attempting—with little evidence—to dismiss TNR under such headings as "The suffering of cats does not end" and "Colony managers often can't manage."[108])

ABC's "Cats Indoors!" campaign shouldn't be dismissed simply as "for the birds." Let's be more explicit. The campaign is not only based on error, jumping too quickly to cite dubious studies, and misreading the substantial literature of previous research. It is also based on an absence of clear and comprehensive thinking, hoping against all reason that feral cats can be adopted into indoor settings in numbers that are wholly unrealistic, or can be handled by the old "trap and remove" strategy that has long since proven a failure, or can be housed in sanctuaries that are not nearly up to the task. (On this last, Alley Cat Allies recently stated, in its new "Glossary of Feral Cat Advocacy Terms," that the "most conservative estimate" of 20 million feral cats in the United States would need "more than 200,000 sanctuaries to house them."[109]) I have to wonder what ABC thinks will save us from those billions of rodents scurrying over our porch railings and scuttling over our sidewalks if feral cats are taken to animal shelters in huge numbers. I also have to wonder how all the journalists could report on this ABC campaign and accept ABC's statements without a quibble or a question. When is a journalist not a careful reporter? When that person is a mouthpiece, even a megaphone, for particular interests, too busy or too lazy to look carefully into the subject.

TROY SNOW

"We believe free-roaming, unowned, and feral cats are entitled to more than the 'right' to death—even if this death is humane."

– Richard Avanzino

TROY SNOW

MEREDITH WEISS

MEREDITH WEISS

KAYE S. COUNCE

TROY SNOW

"The rewards of gaining the trust and affection of these free-spirited animals make it all worth while."

– Dr. Jenny Remfry

TROY SNOW

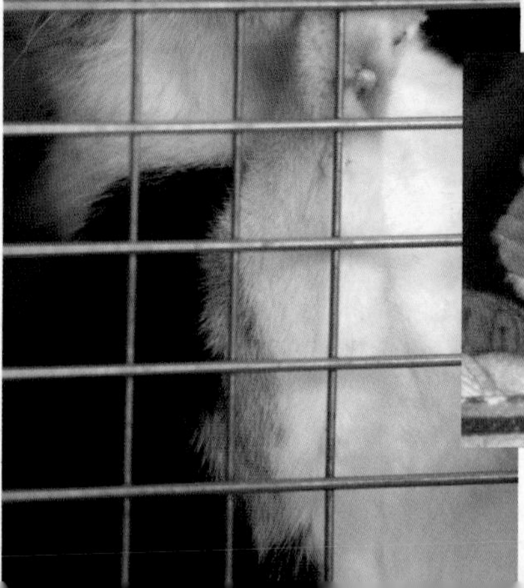

TROY SNOW

SUSAN WOODHOUSE

"As anyone who has cared for feral cats knows, that's what unconditional love is all about."
– Michael Mountain

TROY SNOW

MARIANNE DESAPIO

TROY SNOW

TROY SNOW

TROY SNOW

TROY SNOW

TROY SNOW

TOM DELANEY

TOM DELANEY

"Well-intentioned people argue that it is our humane responsibility to kill ferals kindly, rather than let them face the rigors and perils of an uncertain future. When I observe a recently caught feral cat, cringing in terror in the corner of its cage, I see a being not altogether unlike myself. If I were that feral—facing an immediate, albeit painless death, or a chance at life—replete with all the perilous uncertainties it holds—I would choose life. And so for these ferals, I can choose no less."
– Cole McFarland

TROY SNOW

TROY SNOW

MEREDITH WEISS

TROY SNOW

"I watch George, the former feral, as he lies in the sun—sleek, clean, and at peace with the world—and I know that humane management of feral cats is a noble cause." – June Mirlocca

GEORGE BRINKMAN

"To CFA, every cat is special. But how can you raise the status of cats if your policy is to round up and kill all feral cats?" – Joan Miller

TROY SNOW

KAYE S. COUNCE

TROY SNOW

"TNR (trap/neuter/return) respects a feral cat's wild state ... gives them the opportunity to live among their own, to be free, and to answer to their own unique natures." – NEIGHBORHOOD CATS

CHAPTER **FIVE**

Getting Noticed, Getting Studied

Other organizations revise their stance

But if the American Bird Conservancy is standing firm against TNR, what about other national organizations?

PETA, which has issued new materials on TNR, still remains firmly against TNR. So does the Wildlife Society. In its position statement on "Feral and Free-Ranging Domestic Cats," originally adopted in 2000 and readopted with slight changes in 2002, the Wildlife Society declares strong support for "the humane elimination of feral cat colonies."[110] (Its statement from 2000 supported this humane elimination "within natural areas of importance to native wildlife."[111] Now the humane elimination knows no bounds.) The Wildlife Society is also now in favor of "the passage and enforcement of local and state ordinances prohibiting the public feeding of feral cats," and in opposition to "the passage of any local or state ordinances that legalize the maintenance of 'managed' (trap/neuter/release) free-ranging cat colonies."[112]

Notice the use of the word "release" by the Wildlife Society. (The American Bird Conservancy also uses this word.) While it isn't universally so, it is often true that anyone speaking of "release" is *against* TNR, while anyone speaking of "return" is *for* TNR. Sure enough, here is the Doris Day Animal League, announcing on its website that it "supports the 'trap, neuter, return' method of feral cat population control" (as it has since the early days).[113]

DDAL includes feral cats in its revised manual, *Best Friends for Life: Hu-*

mane Housing for Animals and People, first issued in 1996, then reissued in 2001 in partnership with MSPCA.[114] The new manual broadens its scope in several directions. It now includes advice for people in both federally assisted and privately owned housing, not just people with disabilities only and in assisted housing only. And in its new mention of feral cats (with a description of TNR as "successful" in controlling feral cat populations), the manual gives excellent "soundbites" from Alley Cat Allies and provides addresses and websites for a variety of groups doing TNR.[115]

What about the two groups—American Humane Association and Humane Society of the United States—that originally lent their names to ABC's "Cats Indoors!" campaign? Both AHA and HSUS are still listed in the brochure distributed by ABC. They are listed along with the Pet Care Trust, and these three are the only such organizations to be listed in large type and with their logos.

Does this attribution conform to reality? Not quite. An AHA staff member, telling me that the AHA is no longer linked with ABC in that campaign, sums up AHA's position: "We used to distribute that brochure. We want cats indoors. But the feral cat issue wasn't really addressed."[116] In fact, though, AHA's one-page policy statement on feral cats, unchanged since 1998,[117] can be anything a reader wants it to be. On the one hand, it supports TNR without mentioning TNR by name, calling TNR an interim effort that "may be needed to provide these cats with sterilization, disease prevention, safety and sanctuary." The goal of such programs, states AHA, is "to eventually eliminate feral cat colonies." On the other hand, while AHA "strongly supports policies and programs that work to reduce the overpopulation and abandonment of cats in a humane manner," its statement immediately adds, "In some cases, the most humane solution is euthanasia." These last words have caused Best Friends Animal Society on its website to include AHA among the organizations whose policies it "entirely rejects."[118] AHA, by intention or by oversight, has not made its position clear. An *occasional* euthanasia is surely accepted for the cat too ill or frail to survive even in a managed situation. But *mass* euthanasia is surely rejected by all who advocate the humane and effective alternative of TNR.

The case of HSUS is somewhat different. HSUS departed from the ABC-sponsored campaign by producing its own recent campaign for "Safe Cats"™—i.e., keeping cats indoors. The full packet explaining this campaign, however, still carries the scare-statistic that birds comprise "approximately 25 percent" of the animals killed by free-roaming cats.[119] And the packet still distributes the 1998 statement by HSUS on free-roaming cats, giving what many consider a dubious approval to "TTVARM" as the "more responsibly managed programs" that have recently "supplanted" the "traditional trap, sterilize, and release programs." A new book from the Humane Society Press in 2002, written by veterinarian and epidemiologist Dr. Margaret R. Slater and entitled *Community Approaches to Feral Cats: Problems, Alternatives & Recommendations,* while otherwise providing much good information, continues this unhelpful distinction between TTVARM and TNR.[120]

HSUS wants to be on the right side of things, but doesn't always want to be too much on the side of TNR. In a 2000 issue of its publication *Wildlife Tracks,* the lead article was "Cats and Wildlife."[121] As part of this article, a prominent side-bar on "the feral cat controversy" didn't provide much controversy, listing only the cases where trapping and euthanizing "is the best, and perhaps the only, appropriate strategy."[122] Most of the situations listed were those where any responsible advocate of TNR would also hesitate to recommend TNR.

The American Veterinary Medical Association has had its own second thoughts, presenting a session on "Trap-Neuter-Release" (there's that "release" word again), at its national convention in 2002.[123] Dr. Stanley Temple, a professor in the wildlife ecology department of the University of Wisconsin, warned that cats "can be formidable predators." (He cited his own figures, which have been seriously questioned.) Dr. David Jessup, a senior wildlife veterinarian for the state of California, gave undoubtedly a more serious warning: that by treating a cat and "re-releasing" it, veterinarians "may be violating anti-abandonment laws." Not content with this possibility, Jessup went on to say that "eventually, it's going to end in lawsuits against veterinarians and veterinary associations." Not a comforting message for those attending this convention.

More enthusiastic about TNR is the American Society for the Prevention of Cruelty to Animals. It doesn't yet have a position paper on TNR because its program, beginning late in 2001, is so new. But already ASPCA has a trap bank of about 20 traps, a mobile clinic doing free spay/neuter surgeries for feral cats, and a partnership with several of the most hard-charging local groups. "Everyone who calls, we advise about TNR," says Sandra Sebastian, coordinator of the ASPCA Cares program.[124] And the editor of ASPCA's *Animal Watch,* Marion S. Lane, wrote recently in her opening editorial about five unowned cats that had recovered from their surgery in her laundry room.[125] She was exultant about their prospects: one cat went back to its colony, one ("someone's pet once," she thought, and now testing positive for FIV) stood "a good chance of finding a home for cats with special needs," and three kittens, four months old, went into foster care, there to be tamed and ultimately to be adopted.

Except for a few groups holding out, therefore—or hedging their bets—TNR has been proving itself with the appropriate national and international organizations that now favor this method: World Society for the Protection of Animals (WSPA) which supports TNR at "cat cafés" in tourist hot spots around the world; National Humane Education Society; and Association of Veterinarians for Animal Rights, among others. TNR has already proven itself with the many local groups practicing the humane control of feral cats. But some of TNR's most avid supporters may not know how well TNR has been proving itself with researchers too.

Research on TNR began early

The first study was a Ph.D. thesis undertaken by Paul A. Rees at the University of Bradford in the United Kingdom.[126] (It was supported financially by RSPCA and was completed in 1982.) Investigating the impact of neutering on a specific colony of feral cats, Rees studied the 34 cats on the grounds of a large psychiatric hospital in rural Cheshire. He observed the cats both before and after neutering, and he drew the following conclusions: the neutered cats retained "good condition after neutering"; their social groups were "more stable and better defined"; no new adult males entered the colony; and "no observable changes in behaviour were recorded."[127]

Next was Peter Neville's research on three neutered colonies in Regent's Park and Wandsworth, published in veterinary and pest control journals in the early 1980s.[128] The results were positive, in terms of both the cats and the public agencies concerned with them—TNR presented no difficulties to the cats, and TNR relieved public agencies of continual expenditures for repeat exterminations.[129] Both of these factors have become major components of TNR advocacy.

Roger Tabor's wide-ranging knowledge of the domestic cat—including the feral domestic cat—was apparent in his book, *The Wild Life of the Domestic Cat*, published in 1983.[130] Here, among much else, he described what he labeled the "vacuum effect," whereby new feral cats move into a place emptied of its earlier cats if sufficient food is available to support them.[131] This phenomenon has become one of the strongest arguments against the trap-and-remove approach to control feral cat numbers.

A research report done by Warner C. Passanisi and David W. Macdonald on the "fate" of controlled colonies in the United Kingdom was set up by UFAW and published by that group in 1990.[132] These two respected researchers from the Wildlife Conservation Research Unit of Oxford's Department of Zoology weighed the necessity for control, outlined the various kinds of control, and evaluated eight "neutering and returning" schemes in and around Greater London. Their conclusion: TNR in everyone's view was judged "better than any available alternative," although an objective assessment was impossible because of "the paucity of real data."[133]

Passanisi and Macdonald mentioned, in passing, the "most common complaint" from cat action groups that they had "too few people or too little money" for proper management of colonies,[134] a statement unfortunately used by the American Bird Conservancy to conclude that TNR can't possibly work. But despite this complaint (and despite the admission that one of the evaluated colonies hadn't worked well because of precisely such problems), Passanisi and Macdonald made a series of wide-ranging recommendations about feral cat control that clearly indicated their hope for more—and better—TNR.[135]

In the United States, by the late 1980s, the "consistent failure" of trap-and-remove programs led two veterinarians, Karl I. Zaunbrecher and Richard E. Smith, to study the effectiveness of TNR. They launched their TNR program at a federal research facility and hospital in rural Louisiana and, after three years of study, published their results in the *Journal of the American Veterinary Medical Association* in 1992.[136] Their conclusions: the neutering program was effective (as "demonstrated by the low turnover and improved health of the colony"); the costs were "modest"; and the effect on the institutionalized people who have "long regarded the cats as pets" was highly beneficial.[137] Zaunbrecher and Smith urged a continuation of the neutering program at this hospital in Carville, Louisiana, and a launching of similar programs elsewhere, proclaiming TNR "well-suited to the activities of a volunteer organization."[138]

By the late 1990s, TNR was being practiced frequently enough by such volunteer caretakers for two researchers to study them. Typically, caretakers were assumed to be elderly women, socially isolated, and perhaps a little weird. Not so, according to an investigation done by R. Lee Zasloff and Lynette A. Hart of the Center for Animals in Society at the University of California at

Davis.[139] Their study surveyed people who made frequent use of the Hawaiian Humane Society's free sterilization for homeless/free-roaming/feral cats. The 75 respondents were indeed mostly female but were primarily "middle-aged, living with spouses, well-educated, and employed full time."[140]

Research has now taken off

In the past few years, serious research has expanded considerably, issuing mainly from the University of Florida at Gainesville, appearing in the *Journal of the American Veterinary Medical Association* (*JAVMA*), and listing the name of Dr. Julie Levy either first or second among the researchers. These studies cover a broad range of subjects: the prevalence of FeLV and FIV in unowned free-roaming cats, the use of an anesthetic suitable for neutering feral cats, and the characteristics of unowned cats and their caretakers in various situations and over various lengths of time. The results are exceedingly interesting.

In March 2002, for instance, came news that the incidence of FeLV and FIV in a large group of *unowned* free-roaming cats was similar to the rates reported for *owned* cats.[141] The unowned cats making this history—1,876 of them—were 10 times the number of unowned cats previously tested in the United States for these two infections. Among these 1,876 cats (all from Operation Catnip's TNR programs in Raleigh, North Carolina, and Gainesville, Florida), the overall prevalence of FeLV infection was only 4.3 percent and the overall prevalence of antibodies against FIV infection only 3.5 percent.[142] This finding, by Lee, Levy, et al., suggests that testing for these viruses in a TNR program is unnecessary, thus saving precious resources (time, money, energy) to extend TNR to additional cats.

In May 2002 came an enthusiastic recommendation of the anesthetic combination TKX—used in the neutering of pet cats—for the neutering of feral cats.[143] Since TNR programs are "organized for maximum volume and cost effectiveness" (with up to 12 surgeries performed simultaneously by Operation Catnip, for instance), the anesthetic must have special qualities. It must be "non-technical to prepare and easy to administer to conscious feral cats confined in traps"; induction must be rapid; duration must be predictable; and a low mortality rate must be assured.[144] All of this is supplied by the inexpensive and readily available TKX. Among the 7,502 cats of this study, all from TNR programs in Raleigh and Gainesville, the mortality from anesthesia was only 0.23 percent, which compares well with other anesthetics as reported in studies of small-animal clinics and a teaching hospital.[145] And this low mortality with TKX is all the more promising for feral cats, according to researchers Williams, Levy, et al., considering that the cats in this study "had no physical examination, no laboratory evaluation, an unknown history, sometimes poor body condition, and were often highly stressed prior to anesthesia."[146]

It is especially exciting to see such research coming from Operation Catnip in Raleigh and Gainesville, and from Dr. Levy who began both of these ventures. Not only are these two TNR programs an enormous success in their own right, but the research involving these cats will affect feral cats everywhere.

Here's a subsequent Operation Catnip study—by Centonze and Levy—on the characteristics of free-roaming cats and their caretakers.[147] A written survey drew information from 101 caretakers of 132 colonies in north central Florida—with a total of 920 cats neutered primarily by Operation Catnip. Most of the caretakers (84.6 percent) were women. Their median age was 45 years. Their median household income was $20,000 to $40,000. Married people comprised 52.6 percent of the group; college students, 18.1 percent. A very large number (87 percent) believed that their colonies had a good, or even excellent, quality of life. The caretakers were largely moved to do their work out of "sympathy, affection, or a sense of responsibility for hungry or injured animals," but also out of reluctance to take the animals to an animal control facility for almost certain death.[148] This research concluded, "Recognition of the human-animal bond that exists between caretakers and the feral cats they feed may facilitate the development of effective control programs for feral cat populations."[149] Indeed, stated a different way, as the research also concluded, "If a humane alternative to euthanasia of homeless cats is to be found and implemented, the cooperation of stray and feral cat caretakers is critical and their bond to free-roaming cats should be recognized."[150]

Another study in Florida—by Scott, Levy, et al.—studied the characteristics of 5,323 cats going through a TNR program, showing precisely what can be expected during the neutering aspects of a program.[151] The findings: more spays than castrations were needed; pregnancies varied seasonally from 4 to 47 percent; cryptorchidism appeared in only 1.9 percent of males; prior neutering showed up in only 1.9 percent of cats; general body condition was "adequate"; euthanasia for humane reasons was "quite low" (0.4 percent); unexpected deaths were also low (0.3 percent). The conclusion: "It is feasible and safe to neuter large numbers of free-roaming cats in large-scale clinics."[152]

This last is certainly good news, but it's not exactly hot news for groups that have increasingly been turning to large-scale neutering. It's certainly good news, though, in places like Alachua County, Florida, where, these researchers tell us, "46 percent of the known cat population was unowned, not neutered, and likely contributed the most to local overpopulation."[153]

Most recently, with Julie Levy's primary output, comes an evaluation of a long-term TNR and adoption program.[154] The program had begun in 1991 on the campus of the University of Central Florida, in downtown Orlando, and the evaluation, ending more than a decade later in 2002, had followed the 155 original cats in their 11 managed colonies. These were the results: 47 percent of the cats had been adopted, 15 percent had disappeared, 11 percent had been euthanized, 6 percent had died, and 6 percent had gone into the surrounding woods. This left 15 percent remaining, with no kittens observed on the site after 1995. The researchers concluded that "long-term reduction of free-roaming cat numbers is feasible by TNR" and that an aggressive adoption program can accelerate this decline.[155] However, the immigration of new cats from outside "could substantially limit the success of TNR if an ongoing surveillance and maintenance program is not effective."[156]

This evaluation by Levy, Gale, and Gale must be paired with an M.S. thesis in environmental studies completed in 2001 by Daniel Castillo at Florida International University.[157] His subject: TNR as practiced in two public parks in Miami-Dade County. His purpose: to determine whether managed colonies would decline in size over time, and whether the territorial behavior of cats in established cat colonies would prevent new cats from joining these colonies. His negative conclusions: TNR didn't result in either colony declining in size, and the neutered cats didn't defend their territory against new arrivals.[158] All of this was eagerly picked up by Linda Winter of the American Bird Conservancy as an argument against TNR anywhere and everywhere.

Castillo's exact wording, however, was this: "Even though the number of original colony members decreased over time, illegal dumping of unwanted cats prevented the colonies [at each of the two parks] from decreasing over time." (He noted that these dumped cats were the "primary explanation" for new cats.)[159] In other words, without the dumping, TNR would indeed reduce the size of a colony. But the dumping could probably have been predicted at both of Castillo's sites, and for at least three reasons, according to Cindy

Hewitt, who has trapped at both locations (but isn't a caretaker at either). One: these parks are high-traffic destinations, visited by people in substantial numbers. Two: colony feeders are less than discreet in their efforts (at one of the parks, the cats are fed right alongside the busy marina). Three: major media attention, local and national, has frequently fastened on these colonies, and the result each time has been heavy dumping afterward.[160] Combined, and reinforcing each other, these factors tell irresponsible people precisely where they can, with little guilt, abandon an unwanted cat. And indeed, many cats and kittens are abandoned at A. D. Barnes Park and at Crandon Marina. If these dumped cats were the "primary explanation" for new cats, as Castillo himself noted, isn't it possible that sites less susceptible to dumping would have given TNR a better recommendation? Castillo doesn't ask this question, but we can ask it for him.

Additional refutation of Castillo's work comes from a TNR volunteer who is familiar with this part of Florida.[161] Lynn MacAuley says that food given the cats in these two colonies was overly abundant, and feeding was unmonitored—the colonies were not truly "managed"—and thus a proper measurement of territoriality was impossible.[162] MacAuley observes, further, that Castillo's two locations caused additional problems in making sound deductions about territoriality: one colony was so close to busy city streets that "it is inherently difficult for abandoned or invading cats to be successfully chased off," while the other was on a narrow island (Key Biscayne) from which "it is impossible for 'chased cats' to escape."[163]

Julie Levy, commenting on the Castillo research, sees "one good point… there was minimal hunting"[164]—during all his observations, Castillo saw only two bird-kills. (This interesting fact has apparently gone unnoticed by the bird-minded American Bird Conservancy.) About the Castillo research altogether, Julie Levy says it best: "It should be a lesson for TNR advocates to get their act together."[165] Time and again, proper management is noted as key to proper TNR. The same long-term commitment necessary when adopting a pet is necessary when doing TNR. Managing, monitoring, or maintaining—whatever we call it—is crucial. And proper management, as Alley Cat Allies promotes it, involves even more than a long-term commitment. It involves developing a network—a safety net—of people working together to ensure the continuity of the program beyond the one or two isolated caregivers who may promise their best but, beyond their control, be unable to continue.

Research will only expand

We can expect additional research in the coming years. One interesting study has already been launched by Kimberly B. Subacz, for her M.S. degree in wildlife at Auburn University.[166] On this urban campus in Auburn, Alabama, feral cat colonies have been documented since the 1970s.

The wide-ranging project undertaken by Subacz will be completed by the end of 2004. It will assess the impact of TNR on six previously unmanaged colonies on campus, looking at such factors as population size and density, home-range size, habitat use, and physical health. The investigation will run from one year before neutering until one year afterward, with data coming from examinations of all cats, from surveys of all caretakers, from radio-tracking devices attached to each cat, and from infrared-triggered cameras affixed to each feeding station. This study will also assess 12 previously managed colonies on campus, determining both the size of each population and the rate of immigration of new cats. Subacz is eager to move beyond an anecdotal approval of TNR: "We hope to validate TNR as an ecologically sound and humane method to control populations of feral cats."[167]

Maddie's Fund has research plans regarding feral cats, although not at highest priority. It has already given $9,479,099 to the California Veterinary Medical Association for the first phase of a Feral Cat Altering Program that neutered 170,334 feral cats in three years. Unfortunately, many participating organizations were either unwilling or unable to provide critically important tracking information in a second phase of the project, Maddie's Fund tells me, and thus the second phase was not funded and the project's impact cannot be precisely calculated.[168] The Utah Veterinary Medical Association also received a large Maddie's Fund grant—$353,000 that neutered 4,066 feral cats (and additional animals belonging to low-income residents). Funding of another massive program to neuter feral cats isn't likely from this source.[169] But a "new pilot project," not yet designed, has been envisioned by Richard Avanzino, head of Maddie's Fund, as "intended to more effectively reduce feral cat deaths at animal control facilities."[170] Almost a year later, this project is still on the agenda, I am told, although no details are available on it, and "other urgent and intervening priorities" have prevented work on it.[171] Ultimately the project will be carried out in a "community collaborative program," like all Maddie's Fund projects. And, like all Maddie's Fund projects, it will be awaited eagerly for its imagination, its scope, its eagerness to set a new example, and its hopefulness that there can be better days ahead.

But some of the most interesting research may be exceedingly "low-tech": the effort to gather information locally with the aim of helping the cause of TNR everywhere. The Feral Fix Program of No More Homeless Pets in Utah, for instance, is offering prizes—baseball caps, t-shirts, gift certificates—to all who submit tracking sheets and veterinary records for each feral cat fixed.[172]

Another group seeking to quantify the effectiveness of TNR is Neighborhood Cats, an organization doing TNR in New York City since 1999. In these few years, Neighborhood Cats has begun TNR at these and more: a Bronx jail, a Brooklyn hospital, a Queens clinic, a Staten Island landfill, and many parks and streets on Manhattan's Upper West Side—all five boroughs—and is credited with promoting the rapid growth of TNR throughout the city. As part of its total effort, Neighborhood Cats is working on the creation of an Internet database where caretakers would register their colonies and regularly update their data, and where information would then be available for distribution to interested groups and municipalities across the nation.[173]

Still another group currently collecting data on the impact of TNR is the National Pet Alliance (NPA), based in San Jose, California, and currently doing a follow-up to its 1993 demographic study of cats in Santa Clara County, California. Since 1994, the city of San Jose has supplied vouchers (first at no charge, then at $5) for the spaying and neutering of the area's cats. Anyone who presented a cat was eligible, and a good half of the cats brought in were "stray"—or "stray, feral, loosely-owned and neighborhood," as NPA's Karen Johnson defines that term. Between 1995 and 2000, nine cities in the county, along with the county's humane society, saved almost $3 million because of the decrease in incoming stray cats and owner-surrendered cats.[174] We await the results of the new NPA survey, being conducted by telephone with 1,000 randomly selected households. It should only add weight to the considerable evidence already proving the importance of neutering all cats, both owned and "stray."

Nonsurgical sterilization is on the horizon

Surely some of the most dazzling information affecting TNR, though, in the future, will come from those pursuing the technology of nonsurgical sterilization. In 2000, the Alliance for Contraception in Cats and Dogs (ACCD) was formed, and in 2002 the ACCD held the first International Symposium on Nonsurgical Methods for Pet Population Control. This gathering brought together almost 100 people from 11 countries, to share "ideas, methods, and strategies."[175] Various methods under investigation were considered "promising," and it was thought that we might well see products on the market before long. How long? It was anyone's guess. Several years ago, the estimate was "two to five years."[176] By 2002, it was "by 2010, at the latest,"[177] or "within the next ten years,"[178] according to participants in this symposium. By 2003, the newly approved Neutersol® was in use as a nonsurgical sterilizing agent for male puppies.

Predictions can be "somewhat tricky," according to Dr. Stephen M. Boyle, professor of microbiology at Virginia Tech's Virginia-Maryland Regional College of Veterinary Medicine (and one of the three organizers of the symposium). The technology not only has to work in the lab, it must then be field-tested and subsequently approved by the government. But according to Boyle, field tests for products providing nonsurgical contraception for cats are anticipated "in the next few years."[179]

Another of the symposium's organizers, veterinarian Dr. Henry J. Baker (director of the Scott-Ritchey Research Center at Auburn University's College of Veterinary Medicine), commented on the "troubling" absence of veterinary pharmaceutical firms from the symposium program. But, he noted, these products could get to the market through "other paths"—through small biotechnology firms, for instance, and through university spin-off companies funded by private capital. He then summarized the many features that make contraceptive products less than "sure things" for investors: "1) uncertain acceptance by the veterinary profession; 2) skepticism fueled by past failures of contraceptive products which resulted in long term, serious health problems; 3) relatively low profit margins; 4) lack of a track record to predict FDA regulatory requirements; and 5) lack of experience with 'therapeutic' rather than 'prophylactic' (infectious disease prevention) vaccines."[180] Sounds fairly daunting. Yet dedicated researchers around the world are conducting research with great optimism. Seven foundations in the United States are already funding some of this research or are considering doing so.[181]

What does it all mean for TNR? Feral cats will still need to be neutered, although the neutering process will be simpler and cheaper. Depending on how the contraceptive drugs are administered, trapping may or may not still be required. But the cats will still need to be returned to their colonies, and the colonies will still need to be monitored/maintained/managed. One further certainty, as pointed out by Dr. Brenda Griffin of the Scott-Ritchey Research Center (and the third of the ACCD symposium's organizers): having nonsurgical contraceptive products will mean "addressing the welfare of surplus pets by not allowing the surplus to develop in the first place."[182] So the result will surely be far fewer than the millions of feral cats estimated to be out there now. When *that* will happen is truly anyone's guess.

But before looking at the marvelous future, let's look at the excellent present.

CHAPTER SIX
Achieving Success

TNR is firmly accepted today

We cannot begin to estimate the vast number of feral cats that TNR continues to help.

TNR programs are well-entrenched in many places throughout the United States—college campuses, hospital grounds, prison yards, factory sites, beach areas, marinas, marketplaces, residential neighborhoods, gated communities, and business districts. The locales are urban, suburban, rural. Some TNR programs are relatively new; others began a decade (and more) ago. Some serve only a few alleyways or acres; others are citywide, countywide, even statewide.[183]

TNR is offered in many enticing ways, and often for very little money. The Feral Fix Program of the San Francisco SPCA (SF/SPCA), for instance, which began in 1993, has been a strong influence on the acceptance of TNR, and a role model for numerous programs around the country. In its own program, the San Francisco SPCA has impressively done the following: has offered free health screenings, vaccinations, and spay/neuter surgery for felines in managed colonies; has presented information about feral cats and how to care for them at its week-long "cat camp" (for children aged seven to ten); has held numerous workshops for its caregivers (announced as "the first free, comprehensive training program in the country for cat colony caregivers"); has established Cat Assistance Teams in over a dozen neighborhoods to give advice, moral support, and hands-on assistance such as transportation to the clinic, postsurgical care, and even "colony-sitting" during a caregiver's vacation; and has given a $5 reward to any resident bringing a feral cat for the free surgery—"the only program of its kind anywhere," according to an SF/SPCA ad. Recent economic difficulties have forced this reward to be cut back, but with almost 2,000 feral cats "fixed" every year under the Feral Fix Program, the city of San Francisco has seen its shelter killings reduced to 2.5 per 1,000 residents—lower than any other major city.[184] (Cities the size of San Francisco typically euthanize 10,000 to 25,000 animals a year, says SF/SPCA, while San Francisco is now at an all-time low of euthanizing fewer than 2,000 animals a year.[185])

To the north, the Feral Cat Coalition of Oregon, which began in 1995, outfitted a 24-foot van in 1998 as the nation's first mobile hospital devoted entirely to the neutering of feral cats.[186] The group has no stationary clinic. Its van holds several clinics per month throughout Oregon, neutering at least 3,000 feral cats a year—a total of over 15,000, at last count, without charging caretakers any fee.[187]

In Connecticut, the Mobile Feline Unit of Tait's Every Animal Matters (TEAM)is that state's only mobile spay/neuter clinic. Launched in 1997, it has been on the road at least five days a week, stopping at more than 40 host sites throughout Connecticut and sterilizing almost 60,000 cats in its first six years, one-third of them feral. "Feral cats in traps are welcome aboard the TEAM Mobile Feline Unit," the group advertises. Surgeries for feral cats are done for $30; traps are available for a deposit only.[188]

In Florida, Operation Catnip began using vets in its own clinics when the demand for neutering was too great for the space available in the clinics held every month at the veterinary school. There are now 15 local clinics cooperating with Operation Catnip Outreach in this program. Traps are available on loan from all participating clinics. Caretakers pay only $25 per cat for the surgeries; the rest is paid by Operation Catnip.[189]

And while we're talking money, let's mention some of the excellent financial news that is coming from many areas. The following two, while perhaps not wholly typical, are examples of the possibilities.

San Diego's Feral Cat Coalition (FCC) has been in operation since November 1992. Reporting a decrease of almost 50 percent in cat impoundments and euthanasias by 1997, FCC finds that TNR had saved the municipality nearly $1 million by 1997.[190]

In upstate New York, the Tompkins County SPCA in Ithaca announces that it is "probably the first community in the nation" to kill no feral cats[191]—a situation that began in June 2001 with the start of a TNR program offering free surgeries for feral cats. Going from killing 100 percent of its feral cats to killing none, this organization (under Nathan Winograd's leadership) exchanged a deficit of $150,000 for a surplus of $23,000.[192]

The financing of TNR expands

Still talking money, the funding of TNR programs has been as creative as the programs themselves. We wouldn't be able to count the hundreds of silent auctions, plant sales, yard sales, and wine-tastings (not to mention the thousands of donation cans) that have helped to fund TNR. One organization—Merrimack River Feline Rescue Society, in Massachusetts—runs a successful "Fur-Ball" (!) each year; I would go just for the name. And another group—Forgotten Felines of Sonoma County (FFSC), in California—has run a creative Pick of the Litter Thrift and Gift Shop since 1997. The shop pulls in upwards of $20,000 a month and thus covers the salaries of the few paid staff members at FFSC (a group that has been doing TNR since 1990).[193]

Substantial private grants are also behind TNR. The ASPCA/Fresh Step® Safe Steps Home program, for instance, which began in 2000–2001, had disbursed $155,000 for TNR in its first three years. Seven groups shared this money—Operation Catnip (Florida and North Carolina), Alley Cat Allies, Louisiana SPCA, Neighborhood Cats (New York City), Potter League for Animals (Newport, Rhode Island), and SF/SPCA. This $155,000 for TNR represents 26 percent of all funds given out by the ASPCA/Fresh Step® Safe Steps Home program, the main thrust of which is the support of innovative programs to combat feline homelessness.[194]

PETsMART Charities is also a substantial supporter of feral cat activities. Between early 2000 and late 2003, PETsMART Charities had given 61 grants—individually ranging from $530 to $40,000 and collectively adding up to $610,569—to groups doing TNR. These groups are large and small, well-known across the country and little-known beyond their own township. They span the country—north, south, east, west—from Harbor Humane Society in West Olive, Michigan, to Animal Rescue and Kindness in Warner Robins, Georgia; from Stray Cat Blues in Colmar, Pennsylvania, to Catalyst for Cats in Santa Barbara, California. And the funds cover a wide range of efforts—everything from doing TNR itself, with all its attendant costs (traps, medical equipment, surgeries), to producing educational materials about TNR, and conducting major research.[195] As noted in the PETsMART Charities newsletter of Spring 2003, more than $240,000 was given to TNR recipients in 2002 alone. Further, though, for the year 2002, "Some of the $1.3 million given in other spay/neuter grants also included ferals."

The Geraldine R. Dodge Foundation is another big supporter of TNR, awarding 62 grants since the early 1990s for a total of "approximately $740,000 to address feral cat population issues." The Dodge Foundation approach is four-pronged, with monies going to groups that are national in focus and (within New Jersey) citywide, countywide, and local. On the national level, for example, the Dodge Foundation has funded Alley Cat Allies for distribution of an ACA video in New Jersey. On the statewide level, the Dodge Foundation has, since 1996, supported the Pet Savers New Jersey Feral Subsidy Program with 10 grants (totaling $210,000) to cover the costs of spaying/neutering. On the countywide level, the Dodge Foundation has, since 1990, given nearly $200,000 in support of a model collaboration between Spay, Neuter, and Protect Strays (SNAPS) and the Monmouth County SPCA; in this collaboration, SNAPS traps the cats and monitors their release after surgery, while the SPCA provides the low-cost surgeries. And on the local level, the Dodge Foundation has, since 1994, given more than $300,000 to municipal and private shelters throughout the state to work specifically with the feral cat populations in their communities.[196] (It should also be mentioned that the Dodge Foundation was acknowledged at the outset by the American Bird Conservancy as one of four major funding organizations of ABC's "Cats Indoors!" campaign.)

In addition to these major funding organizations, many smaller foundations in the United States have given their support to TNR over the years, helping groups get started in their own regions, and thereby aiding the growth of the TNR movement throughout the nation. Two foundations of particular significance are Two Mauds, Inc., and the Summerlee Foundation (with the latter supporting not only hands-on work, but also conferences that have brought animal control into the fold).

The above is only a portion of the private grants behind TNR. Increasingly, though, TNR is funded, in part or in whole, by public monies. The TNR program of the Orange County Animal Services, in Florida, for instance, has been funded by the county since 1995, and by 2001 had already saved the county more than $650,000.[197] San Jose, in California, turned over a surplus in animal control funds, plus licensing revenues from dog and cat registration, to support the neutering of cats, both owned and strays. Big savings of public money here too: by 1997, San Jose's annual cost for euthanizing would have been $100,000 greater than the $30,000 spent that year on TNR.[198]

The cities of Berkeley (California), Bridgeport (Connecticut), Folly Beach (South Carolina), Cape May (New Jersey), and Spokane (Washington) are among those funding TNR.[199] Spokane, for instance, passed a "precedent-setting" initiative in 1995 requiring 0.1 percent of the city's general fund to be spent on spaying and neutering animals within the city limits—and these animals included feral cats.[200] Dr. Janet Scarlett, on the faculty at Cornell's veterinary school, makes an important point in regard to public funding: since unowned cats constitute the bulk of shelter killings, she says, after a point it becomes better to invest in sterilizing feral cats than in sterilizing owned cats. "And the municipalities, not the grass roots organizations, have the resources," she adds. "We've got to get them involved."[201] Fortunately, the message is reaching many public officials today that their resources can be best used, for feral cats, by funding TNR programs. Public money for TNR will surely increase.

Some TNR is funded by a combination of public and private monies. Maricopa County in Arizona (which includes fast-growing Phoenix) is considered a promising model for animal control agencies everywhere.[202] While the county's Board of Supervisors has officially endorsed TNR, the county itself does not fund the countywide TNR program called Operation FELIX (Feral Education and Love Instead of eXtermination), which began in 2001. Instead, to perform the spaying and neutering of feral cats, Maricopa County's Animal Care & Control (AC&C) uses funds from the municipalities with which it has contractual arrangements. A private group, Arizona Cat Assistance Teams (AzCATs), works in partnership with AC&C to supply the volunteers, lend the traps, bring in the cats, and teach caretakers the basic requirements of TNR. (With high-volume spay days held almost every week, AzCATs has seen the number of sterilized feral cats rise to more than 500 per month.) Rounding out the funding sources for this rapidly expanding program in metropolitan Phoenix, a recently formed 501(c)(3) charitable organization called Friends of Animal Care & Control supplies funds to cover the various forward-looking programs of AC&C (including Operation FELIX and an outstanding adoption program) that are considered beyond the basic obligations of AC&C.

As word gets out that the TNR method is less expensive than the old trap-and-kill method, public funding everywhere will increase. But however savvy the governments are (and however enlightened the foundations are), we can expect many groups to continue a certain dependence on donations from individuals. The message for concerned individuals, therefore, is clear. We must search the Internet for every possible "link," gather information from every possible source, and give, give, give, to the organization(s) of our choice. Donations of any size are often desperately needed, always gratefully received.

It has been suggested that before a feral cat population can be considered "controlled," at least 70 percent—or even 88 percent—of that population must be sterilized.[203] This will take a lot of money, from every possible source. Very few of us can supply the thousands of dollars to neuter the thousands of cats that will bring us up to the success mark of 70 to 88 percent of the population sterilized. But we can envision our donations as covering one cat at a time, in this effort to reach the many cats needing to be sterilized. That number will be attained one cat at a time, even in a high-speed campaign.

More educational resources are available

The increasing acceptance of TNR can be seen not only in the growing availability of funds but also in the growing availability of educational materials. Written materials came first—excellent products, but from only a few groups, the most prominent of which were Universities Federation for Animal Welfare (in England) and Alley Cat Allies (in the United States).[204] Instructional works have suddenly multiplied, with TNR now advocated and explained in a stack of printed leaflets, guides, manuals, and books.[205]

Classes, too, are now widely offered. Among the best have been the comprehensive workshops given on weeknights and Saturdays as a repeating series by the San Francisco SPCA—information on humane trapping, cat advocacy, neonatal kitten care, socializing feral cats and kittens, feral cat relocation, and feral cat medical issues.

Videos have also carried the message. SF/SPCA did an ambitious multi-tape series for caretakers.[206] Alley Cat Allies did a video for those doing TNR, then did another video for those making the political decisions to do TNR—that is, for those who arrange to approve and fund the TNR that was probably already being done surreptitiously and privately throughout their jurisdictions.[207]

Other tapes are appearing regularly. One such, recently completed, is from San Diego's Feral Cat Coalition—a 43-minute video called *Friends of the Friendless* that offers a "step-by-step guide" to running a "large-scale and low-cost" TNR program, using the high-volume approach that has been so successful for this organization.[208]

Another very interesting video, just completed, is *Working with Feral Cats in Veterinary Practice.* It is for veterinarians, giving them the detailed descriptions and step-by-step techniques for assisting clients in the management of feral cats through TNR. Segments cover these subjects: why TNR is the recommended method of dealing with feline overpopulation; how to trap and hold the feral cat; how to anesthetize and treat the feral cat in veterinary practice; and how to establish and run a large-scale TNR operation. Until now, nothing of this sort has been available for veterinarians. This instructional video, 30 minutes long, is from Auburn University, produced by Whitney Lemarr (class of 2004) and Dr. Brenda Griffin.[209]

Now there's even an Internet course, launched in 2003 by Neighborhood Cats, the energetic TNR group based in New York City.[210] Within its first four months, this Internet course trained more people than the group had reached in two years of live workshops. Some of those trained via this course are from India, Ethiopia, Romania, and other developing nations.

Today, too, almost any organization of any size involved in TNR has its own website. Collectively, these pages do an impressive job of describing the purposes and successes of TNR, and encouraging one and all to "get with the program."

But one of the most recent websites—www.felineresistance—is also one of the best. Begun in 2004, and with content prepared by volunteers who are unidentified, this website sets the record straight on many matters. It addresses "misinformation and lies" of the "Cats Indoors!" campaign of the American Bird Conservancy. It offers assistance to colony caregivers trying to protect their cats from "misguided government action." It delineates various places across the country where TNR is under attack, and it offers suggestions for "fighting back," under categories of "creative resistance, legal action, and pro-active defense." The material is well-presented. Don't miss the "Birds in Cages!" campaign, which Feline Resistance has created as a "fact-based parody" of American Bird Conservancy's "unscientific and disingenuous" campaign aimed at cats.

TNR goes to school

On college campuses, the growth of TNR has been particularly impressive.

The earliest effort was at the University of California at Davis, where a

TNR program was launched in 1986 by the university's Feline Medicine Club (composed of veterinary students).[211] Another early and long-lasting effort in California has been the Stanford Cat Network, which—since 1989—has reduced the feral cat population from an estimated 1,500 to approximately 200 today.[212]

Programs on campuses often begin spontaneously by students and/or faculty members. At the University of Kentucky (UK), for instance, when a student discovered no animal welfare group on campus in 2001, she started her own. The UKSPCA—with a membership that has grown to 80 students—is now actively involved in various activities, including TNR.[213] At the University of Texas at Austin (UT), it took the administration's secret destruction of 14 campus cats during the 1994 Christmas break to galvanize three hardy souls (on campus and in town) to opt for TNR and start the UT Campus Cat Coalition in 1995. Since 1999, no kittens have been born on campus, and the group declares, "We're happy, the administration is happy, and most important of all the *cats* are happy!"[214]

On many campuses, TNR is thriving: a partial list (outdated as soon as it is written) would also include the universities of Washington, Missouri, Texas at San Antonio, and Southern Mississippi, plus Oberlin College, Clemson University, Texas A&M, and North Carolina State University.[215]

One university program has multiple goals. The College of Veterinary Medicine at Auburn University, in Alabama, began a TNR program on campus in 2000, seeking simultaneously to control the feral cat population, to educate students in responsible cat ownership, to add to existing knowledge about TNR, and to give veterinary students the knowledge to conduct TNR programs in their subsequent practices.[216] Notable goals, all.

Veterinary students are increasingly involved. Alley Cat Allies developed a program called Vets for Life, designed to bring vet schools and feral cat caretakers together. (Michigan State and Colorado State were the first two schools to become active in this program, using their spay/neuter rotation to teach TNR and feral cat care to vets-in-training.[217]) And at Cornell, veterinary school students are part of a new program called Cornell-Animal Sterilization Assistance Program (C-ASAP), in which the school is working with nearby shelters to help feral cats, providing examinations, sterilization, and other care.[218]

But on campus, there are still other ways to teach TNR. A full-credit course in "Feral Cat Colony Management" has been offered to University of

California at Los Angeles biology students, with assistance provided by the local Best Friends Catnippers—a group that has acquired its know-how from doing TNR in Los Angeles since the late '90s.[219]

Let me predict that it won't be long before TNR reaches younger students, too, in their after-school activities—going into scout troops, into summer camps (SF/SPCA has already instituted a week-long cat camp), perhaps into Sunday schools—as a way of showing young people the humanitarian and responsible way to treat this group of earth's creatures in need.

CHAPTER SEVEN
Adding It All Up

Successes multiply around the world

Similarly impressive is the growing record of TNR around the world.

The Cats Protection League, founded in 1927 and today calling itself "the oldest and largest charity in the U.K. solely concerned with the welfare of cats and kittens"—also now calling itself Cats Protection—has increasingly been asked to assist with feral cat colonies. It increasingly obliges, by neutering-and-returning-to-site.[220]

Celia Hammond's Animal Trust (CHAT), which opened two clinics in London in the 1990s, notes real improvement in Southeast London and heartening improvement in East London—the latter an area described by CHAT as having "derelict areas not frequented by humans," and cats "on almost every street corner" scavenging for food. "We are contacted about several colonies of feral cats each day," says CHAT.[221] Its policy of acting promptly to neuter feral colonies has greatly reduced the number of calls reporting colonies "of 30, 40 or even 50 cats or more" from areas where such calls were routine only three or four years ago.[222]

As in the case of CHAT, efforts on behalf of TNR are often spurred by the determined efforts of a single person. When an Englishwoman, Vera Davis, visited Spain in 1994 and saw the terrible treatment of feral cats, she returned to the United Kingdom to create the Costa Blanca Feral Cat Trust. Supported now in part by RSPCA and WSPA, the trust organizes visits to villages and mountains of this coastal area of Spain, using makeshift surgeries (a hotel's unused sauna, once) to neuter the feral cats. The hope is to obtain a clinic to carry out a continuing program for the ferals. Meanwhile, videos and leaflets are left with local groups who are happy to see this new approach implemented.[223]

In Venice, the feral cats were so tame they didn't need to be trapped in order to be neutered. Two British women—Helena Sanders and Raymonde Hawkins—first visited Venice in 1965 and soon set up an organization to help the thousands of "cat mothers" who were feeding the street cats there. The help consisted mostly of free veterinary help, often for neutering. Local animal protection societies originally resisted what Jenny Remfry calls "this foreign invasion." But in the end, says Remfry, "the battle was won and neutering schemes for city cats are now accepted in many parts of Italy."[224] In Rome, for instance, the 250 feral cats in the ruins of the Torre Argentina (a tiny fraction of the estimated 200,000 stray cats in the Eternal City) are regularly written up in the cat magazines. These cats and their *gattare*—their "cat ladies"—are finally safe, it would seem; the Torre Argentina Cat Sanctuary recently got official recognition as part of Rome's "bio-cultural heritage."[225] In fact, though, the "wild cats" of Rome have enjoyed special status since 1988, with the passage of Rome's animal rights law. Under this "remarkable" law, the *New York Times* reported, these cats "are guaranteed the right to live where they are born." By 1995, the *Times* could report that 500 colonies (of the city's estimated 10,000 colonies) had been sterilized and were under veterinary supervision.[226]

Canadian efforts owe a huge debt to Lisa McDonald, who began her work in Montreal with Urban Animal Advocates, creating and heading its Feral Cat Program. An early project in Ottawa, neutering a colony of feral cats on the grounds of the Parliament buildings, drew massive and positive media coverage and even a comment from the Speaker of the House of Commons. (Says McDonald: "These ferals had friends in high places!"[227]) Before long, McDonald was helping people all across Canada—among them a veterinarian, Dr. Peter Schwartz, and his feral colonies at several Winnipeg prisons. TNR continues to get good media attention across Canada. Canadians see that the street cats of Saskatoon, the rural cats on the Sunshine Coast of British Columbia, and the prison cats of Manitoba (the prisoners, too) are better off because of TNR.[228]

In Australia, the successful Cats Assistance to Sterilise, Inc. (C.A.T.S.) has "desexed" more than 50,000 wild and tame cats in South Australia in just over a decade.[229] The organization has a growing list of vets eager to help, has decade-long (and longer) records for a lengthy list of feral colonies, and has funds from various governmental bodies who later write enthusiastic letters praising this method of controlling feral cats. Describing the work of C.A.T.S.,

Christine Pierson says that C.A.T.S. tries to establish cooperation among everyone concerned—private groups, government groups, veterinary practices, and individuals. Media response in Australia, too, has been excellent, particularly in the case of the "rock cats" of West Beach (near Adelaide), where a newly elected council in 1994 tried unsuccessfully to destroy a feral cat colony that had been successfully neutered and managed since 1990. It was only a few years ago that a member of Parliament in Australia called for the destruction of all Australian cats. But "zero population," Christine Pierson says, is neither possible nor desirable, "unless one wishes to be overrun with rats and mice."[230] (In fact, this is precisely what happened in Cuba in 1994 when the economic situation caused many Cubans to include felines in their diets. According to an Associated Press news story at the time, a vast proliferation of rodents ensued in the capital city of Havana, "causing health problems."[231])

In South Africa, another ardent supporter of trap-neuter-return is Friends of the Cat (FOC), which was founded in 1991 when the established animal welfare organizations in that country seemed increasingly ready to resort to the "convenience killing" of healthy animals. Says FOC's Geoff Ingham, "The core of the FOC attitude is that feral living is as valid a lifestyle for a cat as [is] domestic bliss with a human family."[232]

TNR is increasingly becoming the chosen method in many parts of the world. In Qatar, the newly formed Qatar Cat Coalition—organized by the faculty at one school—is doing TNR at that school with "great success" and is hoping to branch out to other parts of the city.[233] In Hong Kong, the Hong Kong SPCA has announced its goal of making Hong Kong a "no-kill" city "where no healthy animal will be put to sleep." Reporting this, ASPCA's *Animal Watch* writes that at the heart of this goal is TNR, which was introduced to Hong Kong in 2000 after local SPCA staff had attended a seminar on TNR in the United States[234]

Even in the sensitive environment of the Galapagos Islands, a TNR program has begun—in 2004 in one town, Puerto Villamil, on the largest of the islands, Isabela. The difficult task of getting approval for TNR has been the triumph of Emma Clifford, whose accomplishments have also included the management and expansion of the SF/SPCA feral cat program. Clifford's Animal Balance is working with various segments of the Galapagos community (governmental, business, and residential). Using surgical equipment donated to the Galapagos National Park Service, the program hopes to "pass the torch to the local community," as Clifford states it, and move TNR to the next island. "Our hope"—in Clifford's words—is not only to manage the feral cats of the Galapagos, but also "to generate a model that could be replicated around the world."[235]

TNR efforts around the world will often be difficult. The Cat Welfare Society of Israel (CWSI) for instance, begun by Rivi Mayer in 1990, introduced TNR to that country.[236] Fresh from her military service, Mayer wanted to set up a boarding cattery, and she traveled to England for advice. There she met Peter Neville, and she returned to Israel in 1986 well-equipped to start doing TNR. It was a "very, very strange notion at that time," she recalls, since no feline welfare existed in Israel. Mass poisoning of feral cats was routine. The first city veterinarian to understand TNR was Dr. Zvi Galin, of Tel Aviv, around 1994. Because of his activities, the veterinary association brought him up on charges and fined him. He resigned, refusing to pay. (He has since been asked to rejoin and even give lectures!) Fully supportive of TNR—and providing some funds—is the Ministry of Environment. And the Ministry of Agriculture is "reluctantly beginning to acknowledge that TNR is a fact of life," sometimes helping with rabies vaccine, says Ellen Moshenberg, a CWSI volunteer and representative. CWSI is active not only in sterilizing feral cats (80,000 done directly by CWSI or by vets sponsored partly or wholly by CWSI); the organization is also active in lobbying governmental entities and in educating the many grass-roots groups of feeders. Many trimmed left ears are visible today in Tel Aviv and other cities. Unfortunately, CWSI today is in "desperate" need of funds, a situation that has virtually halted the TNR program in the city of Arad, a program assisted, in part, by CWSI. "We did about 2,000, which was not nearly enough, and right now we are almost back to where we were," says Moshenberg, who lives in Arad. It's an up-and-down struggle, in some of these countries—changing minds, getting money, and keeping up with the enormous job to be done.

On the international front, however, the Marchig Animal Welfare Trust, in Scotland, has been funding TNR since that trust was established in 1989. The Marchig Trust works on a wide variety of projects—running anti-fur and anti-poaching campaigns, seeking alternatives to the use of animals in research, funding spay/neuter programs and mobile clinics, establishing sanctuaries, and assisting in the formation of groups committed to the cause of animal welfare. According to Les Ward of the trust, "some of the groups receiving Marchig grants for TNR programs have been Fethiye Hayvan Dostlari Dernegi in Turkey, Sicilian Cat Welfare Society in Sicily, Friends of the Ferals and the Costa Blanca Feral Cat Trust in Spain, and Friends of the Cat in Greece."[237] (The trust's website—www.marchigawt.org—reveals a number of other groups, worldwide, whose work in TNR will be familiar.) While precise amounts, or even rough totals, could not be obtained from the Marchig Trust, it is clear that this source of funds is a boon to TNR efforts throughout the world, especially with the trust's current priority of helping the developing world.

Some disagreements can be noticed

Among those practicing TNR, differences of opinion will occasionally surface.

In South Africa, for instance, Friends of the Cat has perhaps hit a nerve in defending relocation. But after more than a decade of close involvement with feral cats, Geoff Ingham of FOC strongly defends the release of neutered feral cats to new territories, having concluded that "a healthy feral is generally more than capable of adapting to life in a new territory."[238] FOC argues against what it calls UFAW's "human-oriented" preference for euthanasia in cases where the only other possibilities are relocating the cats or leaving them without long-term management.[239]

Another situation that might favor euthanasia over TNR comes from recent research by David W. Macdonald, Nobuyuki Yamaguchi, and Warner C. Passanisi of Oxford's Department of Zoology.[240] The subject of their study, sponsored by UFAW, was a colony of 50 to 80 feral cats on a farm in Oxfordshire. Discovering that Peripheral Females are "likely to be in poor health" compared to Central Females and to Peripheral and Central Males, these researchers suggest that "euthanasia may be a better welfare option for this class of cat."[241]

Disagreements occur on other matters. Some want all caretakers to be registered; others oppose any such official listing. Some insist upon full testing—for feline leukemia virus, feline immunodeficiency virus, or "any other chronic or debilitating disease," as HSUS states it.[242] Others do not advocate such testing, basing their decision on the almost identical incidence of FeLV and FIV among feral and owned cats, on the high rate of false positives in FIV tests (about 20 percent), and on the low rate of FIV-positive cats that actually come down with the disease (about 10 percent).[243] With such statistics available, some people prefer to eliminate testing and proceed instead with additional TNR—"overpopulation kills more cats than any disease," as Alley Cat Allies has expressed it.[244]

Perhaps this matter of testing will, in the future, be as uncontroversial as the matter of eartipping is today. Once considered a form of mutilation, eartipping is now widely accepted: a clear indication of a cat that has already been neutered and needn't be trapped anew. Indeed, many a caretaker will look with pleasure upon a colony of mostly (or completely) eartipped cats and therefore a job mostly (or completely) done. The small piece taken from the ear is seen as positive, not negative.

These differences—singly or together—do not indicate an irremediable split in this movement. Rather, they indicate a freedom of thought in a movement whose members have far more in common with each other than they do with anyone seeking to eradicate feral cats by killing them. For the TNR movement has spread around the world because like-minded people have rebelled against the wrong-headedness—the failure, quite apart from anything more subjectively judgmental—of the trap-and-kill effort.

The evidence runs solidly against trap-and-kill

Predator-eradication programs can backfire in numerous ways. On Amsterdam Island, in the Indian Ocean, cat-eradication efforts to protect the island's ground-nesting birds immediately (and vastly) increased the number of black rats and house mice, which then preyed immediately (and vastly) on the birds.[245] Closer to home, in Ventura, California, the rounding up of feral cats in the late '90s is seen as contributing to the hordes of rats infesting the public beaches several years later.[246] (In downtown Los Angeles, operators of the flower market recently found a solution to their rat problem; they introduced "a pride of feral cats"—neutered, of course—and now find that the place "never looked cleaner, rat-wise."[247])

But cat-killing has additional consequences beyond the increase in rodents, which are easily more disease-bearing than any cats, in addition to being potentially as bird-killing. The expensive efforts to eradicate cats must be repeated again and again and again, since new cats will constantly move into a vacated habitat to take advantage of its continuing food supply. A fact that needs to be pounded home about the "vacuum effect," which draws cats into an area emptied of its previous cats, is that an area's food supply is not only what human beings provide but also, to a significant extent, what nature provides. Even if people weren't providing food, the cats would still be there, getting sustenance from other food sources in the territory. These sources may not be adequate, and the cats may suffer greatly, but they will remain in their territory. If the cats were removed, the vacuum effect would draw other feral cats into such an area, constantly frustrating the trap-and-kill advocates. Lethal measures, therefore, not only "fail to take into consideration the immense affection the public has for homeless animals," as Dr. Levy has stated.[248] (In Florida's Alachua County, for instance, unowned cats are being fed by a very high 12 percent of households.[249]) Lethal measures also fail to consider the natural food sources that are available to the cats—food that cannot be withheld by municipal ordinance.

The arguments are strong for TNR

TNR has many solid and measurable advantages, as already mentioned. A drop in the euthanasia rate, following the energetic pursuit of TNR. A decrease in complaints, as the need for male cats to roam and spray and fight is reduced. A reduction in public expenditures for animal control.

But not all of the arguments for TNR can be measured so precisely. The continued presence of cats, for instance, could be giving birds a little-mentioned benefit. The outstanding Paul Leyhausen, whose early studies of cat behavior are still so significant, poses this possibility: "Feral cats may even serve the health of singing bird populations in such urban and other areas where the indigenous bird and egg hunting predators have been drastically reduced numerically or even extinguished, since a certain degree of predation is necessary to keep wild animal populations in good health and condition."[250]

Researchers have attempted to measure what motivates people to undertake TNR. In their study of 101 caretakers, Lisa A. Centonze and Julie K. Levy found that TNR was chosen overwhelmingly for one reason: 76.6 percent of these caretakers didn't want the cats to be killed.[251] These caretakers in Florida had a strong bond with their feral cats. The bond was "different from the traditional image of the human-animal bond," but arose from some of the same factors: a combination of sympathy, affection, and ethical concern. (In fact, 66 percent of these caretakers were already cat owners.) A previous survey of caretakers, by Zasloff and Hart, found that 64 percent of their 75 caretakers in Hawaii answered "yes" to the question "Do you consider the cats to be 'yours'?" The main reasons for the "remarkable commitment" of the Zasloff and Hart caretakers appeared to be "love of cats, opportunity for nurturing, and enhanced feelings of self-esteem."[252]

Many of the arguments for TNR, however, defy measurement altogether. Jenny Remfry, mentioning the difficulties encountered by caretakers—difficulties with the public, with each other, and with their own energy and bank accounts—concludes, nevertheless, that "the rewards of gaining the trust and affection of these free-spirited animals make it all worth while."[253] Michael Mountain, one of the founders of Best Friends Animal Sanctuary, articulates it splendidly: "as anyone who has cared for feral cats knows, that's what unconditional love is all about."[254]

For Nathan Winograd, who has been actively involved in TNR—first at Stanford University, then at SF/SPCA, then at Tompkins County SPCA in upstate New York—there are four good reasons to do TNR: it's effective, easy, humane, and "you'll be in good company," joining "tens of thousands of compassionate people" already helping feral cats in this way.[255] It is Winograd who argues (along with many others) that cats in managed colonies "often lead long contented lives,"[256] giving the lie to those who contend that feral life is too nasty, brutish, and short to be encouraged.

Perhaps one of the people attending the AHA scientific workshop in 1996 summed it up best. Seeing one of her ferals, George, "as he lies in the sun—sleek, clean, and at peace with the world," she knows that TNR is "a noble cause."[257]

There are additional benefits, though. In a 1996 article in *JAVMA*, Jane Mahlow and Margaret Slater state that "another argument for sterilize-and-release programs is that stray and feral cats may not always be unwelcome"—a delicate reference to the heavy rodent infestations that may occur, for instance, in factory areas.[258]

And for still others, the reasons are philosophical. Neighborhood Cats (operating in the heart of New York City) refers to TNR as respecting "a feral cat's wild state" and as recognizing "a new balance in our urban and rural landscape, one that includes feral cats."[259]

Yet for the predictable future, we'll undoubtedly keep hearing the tired arguments against TNR—against sterilizing feral cats and maintaining them in their original colonies as the best way to control their numbers and their impact.

One of these tired arguments is that TNR is a hardship to the cats. That death would be better. Don't expect anyone closest to the cats—their caregivers—to agree with this one! Cole McFarland, then managing director of the

Labette Humane Society in rural Kansas, wrote eloquently on this question in the early 1990s: "Well-intentioned people argue that it is our humane responsibility to kill ferals kindly, rather than let them face the rigors and perils of an uncertain future. When I observe a recently caught feral cat, cringing in terror in the corner of its cage, I see a being not altogether unlike myself. If I were that feral—facing an immediate, albeit painless death, or a chance at life—replete with all the perilous uncertainties it holds—I would choose life. And so for these ferals, I can choose no less."[260] McFarland's words remain compelling.

Another of the all-too-familiar arguments is that TNR is a threat to wildlife. Among the groups most prominently making this argument are the Wildlife Department of the HSUS, the National Wildlife Rehabilitators Association, the International Wildlife Rehabilitation Council, and the Fund for Animals. Their argument is simple: feral cats are invasive predators and must be removed. But the predator-prey relationship is not so simple. Those who propose the removal of feral cats either do not recognize or do not credit the following factors: 1) predators promote the health of their prey populations by killing off the less able members of those populations; 2) predators are themselves regulated by their prey—as a prey population rises and falls, according to its natural population regulation cycles, a predator population will also rise and fall; and 3) the removal of a predator does not guarantee that the prey population won't be under similar or greater pressure from other predators adapting to the newly changed environment.

Failing to understand predation is not the only problem. Making judgments is another. As biologist Roger Tabor has noted, "Almost incredibly, in the USA there is a growing idea that carnivores are somehow immoral."[261] However, in a neat rejoinder to all such simplistic or wishful thinking about predation, Neighborhood Cats replies that the statistics cited by the wildlife worriers are totally beside the point—whether these numbers are accurate or exaggerated isn't important—because without TNR there would be even *more* feral cats and an even larger impact on the cats' prey! A great argument for our side! As Neighborhood Cats states it, "We need to point out, again and again, that ultimately the wildlife and TNR organizations want the same thing—fewer feral cats. The wildlife groups have no realistic way to get there. We do."[262]

Still another of the scary arguments is that TNR is a threat to human beings. In Singapore, the fear that cats might spread Severe Acute Respiratory

Syndrome (SARS) has led to the shutting down of the five-year-old Stray Cat Rehabilitation Scheme sponsored by Singapore's Agrifood and Veterinary Authority. This, despite the fact that tests have found no such link between cats and this frequently lethal disease (and despite the additional fact that sterilizing even a fraction of Singapore's homeless cats has led to a continual lowering of the number of homeless cats). But don't bother anyone with the facts. In Singapore, it's back to rounding up and killing feral cats, at least for a while.[263]

In the United States, the fear that cats might spread rabies to human beings can be dispelled in an instant by statistics from the Centers for Disease Control and Prevention (CDC). In the years from 1990 to 2002 (the last year for which figures are currently available), a total of only 36 deaths from rabies occurred in the United States, with 7 of them having originated in other countries, and none of them having come from a cat.[264] As shown in the detailed mortality reports from CDC, bats are overwhelmingly responsible for these 36 cases,[265] which, in any case, are only a fraction of the United States deaths from rabies in decades past.[266]

A far more lethal threat to people would be the immediate rise in rodent numbers—and the consequent rise in bubonic plague and hantavirus disease—which would follow the sudden removal of all feral and free-roaming cats, whether by trapping-and-euthanizing, by poisoning, by infecting with lethal diseases, or by shooting, all of which methods have been tried and advocated around the world as quicker fixes than the real fix of TNR. In addition to every other advantage offered by the alternative of TNR (its humaneness, its effectiveness, and its economy), its slower winding-down of feral cat numbers can allow hawks, owls, and other natural predators of rodents to adapt to a changing situation and keep their rodent populations under control.[267] Let's not let cats be feared in a false panic about their bringing rabies to humans, while allowing rodents to be overlooked in a dangerous calm about *their* potential for harm.

The list of arguments against TNR goes on. That TNR attracts more cats, eager for the food provided by a colony's caretaker;[268] this can happen, of course, but a well-managed colony will get only the food it needs, with nothing left behind. Or that TNR invites irresponsible people to dump their unwanted cats at the site of a managed colony;[269] this, too, can happen, but a well-managed colony will have any newcomers neutered.

One more argument is often raised: that TNR is an impossible task considering the numbers of cats involved and the funds and people required.[270]

Those who are doing the work, however, know its value, both for the individual cats and for the overpopulation problem. The work will continue. It will grow.

It will often be a struggle—with bureaucracies, with the media, with politicians, with organizations, with anyone who does not want to be bothered by ideas or facts that are new to them. There will be triumphs. There will be disappointments. The disappointments of one day may well become the triumphs of another day. Those who do not despair at the disappointments—those who take heart from the triumphs—know that the solid commitment and unflinching devotion behind TNR will only continue. The TNR movement will only grow.

Notes

1. Jenny Remfry, *Ruth Plant: A Pioneer in Animal Welfare* (Barnet, Herts.: Remfry, 2001), 49.

2. Celia Hammond, "Long Term Management of Feral Cat Colonies," in *The Ecology and Control of Feral Cats* (Potters Bar, Herts.: Universities Federation for Animal Welfare, 1981), 89.

3. Celia Hammond, letter to Ellen Perry Berkeley, 23 April 2003, clarifying a confusion about dates in material published elsewhere.

4. Celia Hammond, "Long-Term Management of Feral Cat Colonies," in *The Ecology and Control of Feral Cats*, op. cit., 89.

5. Ibid., 89.

6. Jenny Remfry, *Ruth Plant*, op. cit., 9, 24–25, 37, 88.

7. Ruth Plant, letter to Ellen Perry Berkeley, 17 November 1983.

8. Margaret Uppal (Joint Chair, Cat Action Trust 1977), letter to Ellen Perry Berkeley, 2 August 1999.

9. Jenny Remfry, letter to Ellen Perry Berkeley, 24 April 1999.

10. *Annual Report, 1980–1981,* Universities Federation for Animal Welfare, 13.

11. Tom Kristensen, "Feral Cat Control in Denmark," in *The Ecology and Control of Feral Cats*, op. cit., 68–72.

12. Ibid., 70.

13. Jenny Remfry, *Ruth Plant*, op. cit., 75.

14. Jenny Remfry, "Strategies for Control," in *The Ecology and Control of Feral Cats*, op. cit., 73–79.

15. Ibid., 75.

16. Ibid., 75–78.

17. Ibid., 75.

18. Ibid., 75. This was almost a quarter of a century ago. The TNR movement has evolved considerably since then, and some of its earliest recommendations—such as incomplete neutering of a colony—are no longer part of the movement today.

19. Roger Tabor, "General Biology of Feral Cats," in *The Ecology and Control of Feral Cats*, op. cit., 5–11.

20. Ibid., 9. But Tabor saw the possibility of problems in neutering-and-returning-to-site in urban locations, and he agreed with Remfry that not all breeding should be eliminated in a neutered colony. Speaking in the Open Forum at the end of the UFAW symposium, Tabor is summarized as saying, "Once the established cats began to die, new cats would enter the colony, the degree of cohesiveness would be lost and strays would find it easier to 'gate-crash'; thus the control of the colony would be less effective. Perhaps it would be preferable to allow a low level of breeding in the original family groups in order to produce some long term continuity."

21. Ellen Perry Berkeley, *Maverick Cats: Encounters with Feral Cats* (hardcover, New York: Walker & Company, 1982; paperback, Shelburne, VT: New England Press, 1987; expanded and updated edition, Shelburne, VT: New England Press, 2001), 159 pages.

22. Oliphant F. Jackson (Chairman of the Working Party), *Feral Cats in the United Kingdom: Report of the Working Party on Feral Cats, 1977–1981* (Horsham, Sussex: Royal Society for the Prevention of Cruelty to Animals: 1981), 11.

23. Jenny Remfry, *Ruth Plant*, op. cit., 50.

24. *Feral Cats in the United Kingdom*, op. cit., 27.

25. Ibid., 11.

26. Ibid., 10.

27. Ellen Perry Berkeley, "Controlling Feral Cats: Officials in England Are Experimenting with a Uniquely Effective and Humane Way of Controlling Feral Cat Populations," *Cat Fancy* (September 1984), 16–19.

28. Ibid., 17. *See also*: Peter F. Neville and Jenny Remfry, "Effect of Neutering on Two Groups of Feral Cats," *Veterinary Record* 114 (1984), 447–450.

29. *UFAW News-Sheet*, a publication of Universities Federation for Animal Welfare (August 1983), 6.

30. Peter F. Neville, "Humane Control of an Urban Cat Colony," *International Pest Control* (September/October 1983), 144–145, 152.

31. Peter Neville, letter to Ellen Perry Berkeley, 16 April 2002.

32. Peter Neville, letter to Ellen Perry Berkeley, 12 February 2001.

33. Jenny Remfry, *Ruth Plant*, op. cit., 53–54.

34. Ellen Perry Berkeley, "Feral Cats: Across the Country, People Are Working to Humanely Control Feral Cat Populations," *Cat Fancy* (July 1990), 20–27.

35. Ibid., Joanne Bruno (a founder of Animal Umbrella, E. Arlington, MA), 26.

36. For information on the various programs and publications of Alley Cat Allies, write to the organization at 1801 Belmont Road NW, Suite 201, Washington, DC 20009-5147, or call 202-667-3630, or log on to www.alleycat.org.

37. *Alley Cat Action*, a publication of Alley Cat Allies (Winter 2001), 1, 4.

38. Michael J. Konecny and Barbara Sleeper, "When Tabby Leaves Home: Cats That Walk on the Wild Side Face, and Pose, Serious Threats," *Animals*, a publication of the Massachusetts Society for the Prevention of Cruelty to Animals (November/December 1987), 12–17.

39. Here are only a few of the errors. 1) The Konecny-Sleeper figure of 31 million feral cats in 1972 (supposedly from William George) is incorrect; even a casual reading of George's work reveals that his estimate referred to all cats in the United States, not just to feral cats. 2) The Konecny-Sleeper claim of feral cat density reaching "7,400 cats per square kilometer in dockyard and industrial neighborhoods in Baltimore" is totally incorrect; I tracked this figure to a doctoral dissertation by Peter Apps (who admitted to me that he had made a mistake in converting hectares to kilometers, and that the correct figure should have been 740 cats per square kilometer for the Baltimore dockyards, not an unusual figure for such a situation). 3) The Konecny-Sleeper claim that the Galapagos cats studied by Konecny had shown unusual behaviors, not reported elsewhere, is sloppy; the behaviors cited in the article—communal foraging and paternal care of kittens—had been observed by Peter Apps on Dassen Island, off the coast of South Africa, had been described by that researcher, and had been reported by me in *Maverick Cats*. 4) The Konecny-Sleeper report of a 3:1 ratio of males to females on two islands of the Galapagos, as supposedly mirroring the population structure of feral cats "on other islands" (in the Galapagos? elsewhere? unclear), is inadequately explained; male-biased sex ratios are not by any means typical of island cat populations, as the literature plainly shows. (If found in any cat populations, such skewed sex ratios are most likely due to sampling bias, it is thought, since males move around more than females and are therefore seen more.) 5) The Konecny-Sleeper statement that in the southern Pacific and Indian oceans "cats showed a marked preference for birds such as petrels,

penguins, and cormorants" is misleading. The cats on these islands do not have a choice as to what they can eat. Birds are there; other prey is not. 6) The Konecny-Sleeper assertion that cats "pose a serious threat to some endemic species" on the Galapagos does not mention that rats would appear to be the primary predators of certain endangered ground-nesting birds on these islands (a fact brought out in a documentary on the Galapagos that aired on public television in the late 1980s—a documentary, incidentally, that mentions feral cats only in passing).

40. Michael J. Konecny and Barbara Sleeper, "When Tabby Leaves Home," op. cit., 17.

41. Rhonda Lucas Donald, "Should Feral Cats Be Euthanized?" *Shelter Sense*, a publication of The Humane Society of the United States (May 1992), 3–7. The first misleading statement by Donald is a description of UFAW's 48-page "research report" as a "booklet." (The research had been conducted by highly qualified researchers in Oxford University's Department of Zoology—Warner C. Passanisi and David W. Macdonald—see note 42 below.) Donald then gives an incomplete explanation of the research findings. And a major recommendation of the UFAW research, that a "national centre for the management of feral cat populations" be established, is omitted altogether. Would this "centre"—intended to explain the benefits of TNR, to supply traps, to keep records, and to train people in carrying out a control scheme—be advocated by a research project that had found anything other than what researchers Passanisi and Macdonald had found? Here's a key statement from the conclusion of their UFAW report: "Virtually everyone involved in cat control who was interviewed during this study commented that neutering schemes have worked better than any available alternative might have done."

42. Warner C. Passanisi and David W. Macdonald, *The Fate of Controlled Feral Cat Colonies, UFAW Animal Welfare Research Report No. 4* (Potters Bar, Herts.: Universities Federation for Animal Welfare, 1990), 48 pages.

43. Ibid., 42.

44. Rhonda Lucas Donald, "Should Feral Cats Be Euthanized?" op. cit., 5.

45. Ibid., 4. Preceding the Rhonda Lucas Donald article was a full-page editorial comment written by Marc Paulhus, vice-president for companion animals at HSUS. His words left no doubt as to the HSUS position on "neuter-and-release" efforts. According to Paulhus, such programs are "misguided," they do not approach the problem either "realistically" or "compassionately," and they "amount to nothing more than subsidized abandonment."

46. Charles E. Samarra (chief of police, Alexandria, VA), memo to Mayor Patricia S. Ticer, 21 July 1995.

47. Louise Holton, telephone message to Ellen Perry Berkeley, undated.

48. *A Critical Evaluation of Free-Roaming/Unowned/Feral Cats in the United States: Proceedings of a Scientific Workshop Sponsored by the American Humane Association and the Cat Fanciers' Association* (Englewood, CO: American Humane Association, 1997), 73 pp. For a copy of this $13 report, call American Humane at 800-227-4645, or visit the website www.americanhumane.org, or write to American Humane, 63 Inverness Drive East, Denver, CO 80112.

49. Ibid., Dorothy Hyde (Corvallis, OR), 64.

50. Ibid., Diane F. East (a founder of Animal Advocates, N. Dartmouth, MA), 48.

51. Ibid., Richard Avanzino (then president, San Francisco SPCA, San Francisco, CA), 16.

52. Ibid., W. Marvin Mackie (owner and director, Animal Birth Control, San Pedro, CA), 49.

53. Ibid., Karen Johnson (National Pet Alliance, San Jose, CA), "Four Study Comparison," 57.

54. Paula Abend and Karyn Miller-Medzon, "Stray Cats, Friends in Need: Free-Roaming, Lost, or Stray, that Cat on the Street Needs Your Help," *Animals*, a publication of the Massachusetts Society for the Prevention of Cruelty to Animals (July/August 1995), 26–29, 36.

55. Carter Luke, "Guidelines for Cat Rescue," *Animal People* (June 1993), 9. The guidelines (on neuter/release, adoption, and euthanasia) are published in their entirety in this issue.

56. "Vets Talk about Low-Cost Neutering," *Animal People* (July/August 1994), 5. Further questions, in this survey done by *Animal People* for SPAY/USA, are also interesting. Should low-cost neutering be restricted to owned pets? No, said 66 percent. Should a national low-cost neutering program be set up to aid neuter-and-release programs? Yes, said 41 percent.

57. Jenny Remfry, "Feral Cats in the United Kingdom," *Journal of the American Veterinary Medical Association* 208:4 (15 February 1996), 520–524.

58. "AVMA Adopts Position on Abandoned and Feral Cats," *Journal of the*

American Veterinary Medical Association (15 September 1996), 1042–1043. The AVMA's "minimum requirements" for "managed colonies," adopted by the AVMA's Executive Board on 19 July 1996, are published in their entirety in this article.

59. Joan Miller, telephone interview with Ellen Perry Berkeley, 4 February 1999.

60. Ibid.

61. "CFA Board Takes Stands," press release from the Cat Fanciers' Association, undated. The guidance statement on free-roaming/unowned/feral cats, adopted by the CFA Board of Directors on 7–8 February 1998, is published in its entirety in this press release.

62. "Free-Roaming Cats: In Search of New Approaches; Crafting Solutions," *Animal Sheltering*, a publication of The Humane Society of the United States (September-October 1998), 15.

63. Ibid., 17.

64. Ibid., 18.

65. See text, section entitled "Research has now taken off," and notes 136–137 below.

66. Gary J. Patronek, letter to Ellen Perry Berkeley, 4 January 1999.

67. Stephen Zawistowski (science advisor to ASPCA and chairman of NCPPSP's Science Advisory Committee), telephone interview with Ellen Perry Berkeley, 4 April 2003; and Margaret R. Slater (principal researcher in this NCPPSP project), letters to Ellen Perry Berkeley, 7 April and 28 April 2003, and 15 February 2004. This research, still in the planning stages, has been variously described by these two as "the next step beyond TNR," and as "preceding TNR," and as a project that "does not address TNR directly in any way."

68. Jane Musgrave, "America's Five Best Kitty Cities: Where Cats Are More Than Welcome," *Cat Fancy* (October 2001), 22–29. (The five cities are San Francisco, CA; Austin, TX; San Diego, CA; Orlando, FL; and Denver, CO.)

69. Kim Bartlett, "Rethinking Neuter/Release," *Animal People* (June 1993), 8. *See also*: Merritt Clifton, "What We've Learned from Feral Cats," *Animal People* (June 1993), 1, 7–8; and Merritt Clifton, "Until There Are None, Spay/Neuter One," *The Animals' Agenda*, a publication of The Animal Rights Network (May 1992), 12–19.

70. Merritt Clifton writes this, in "Gains against Pet Overpopulation Come as Others Seek Basic Services," *Animal People* (November 1997), 16: "Through the advent of high-volume, low-cost neutering, and the largely self-financed work of thousands of local rescue and neuter/release volunteers, the number of animals entering United States and Canadian animal shelters may be at a 70-year low." Within four years, he would write this, in "Gains and Casualties in the No-Kill Revolution," *Animal People* (July/August 2001), 11: "Low-cost and free sterilization, neuter/return feral cat control, improved pet identification, and high-volume adoption have cut the numbers of animals killed in shelters by 75% in just 15 years."

71. Merritt Clifton, "'Rescue' Should Not Perpetuate the Problem," *Animal People* (June 2002), 3. Not everyone shares Clifton's optimism. ACA's Becky Robinson tells me that his picture of great progress "does not hold up in our daily experience with shelters and animal control agencies." In her message to me (23 January 2004), she continues: "Complaints about cats are as high or higher than ever in areas where TNR is not comprehensively practiced. We hear from shelters that they are getting more cats, more complaints about cats, and more problems related to cats. . . . Some of the causes of this are increased human population, our transient society (more people moving and leaving their animals), and fewer rental properties that allow cats."

72. Merritt Clifton, "Where Cats Belong—and Where They Don't," *Animal People* (June 2003), 16. Interestingly, Clifton notes that the feral population has been further reduced by taming and adoption. "Up to a third of all pet cats now appear to be recruited from the feral population," he writes in this article.

73. Merritt Clifton, "Feral/Outdoor Cats & Roadkill Data," e-mail to Ellen Perry Berkeley (and to all others who had been in contact with *Animal People* about feral cats during the previous 18 months), 21 October 2003. The effort to keep pet cats indoors has also helped to reduce the feral cat population, Clifton says, in this message, "but the magnitude of the drop is such that the sterilization effort clearly has the most to do with it." A month later, discussing feral cat numbers and the causes of feral cat mortality—chiefly, the drop in roadkills and the increase in predation (by coyotes in particular)—Clifton suggests that the population of feral cats in the United States "may have been reduced to as few as five million." *See*: Merritt Clifton, "Roadkills of Cats Fall 90% in 10 Years—Are Feral Cats on Their Way Out?" *Animal People* (November 2003), 1, 8. While many people are elated about this recent drop in feral cat numbers, others—such as Becky Robinson of Alley Cat Allies—are skeptical. Questioning the

roadkill figures, for instance, Robinson mentions that "it has only been in recent years and only in some areas that killed animals were tabulated by species." She is probably not alone in questioning this newest figure of feral cat numbers ("as few as five million"), which comes so soon after Clifton's previous estimate of almost three times that number ("as low as 13 million").

74. Alex Matthews, *Cat's Claw* (Philadelphia: Intrigue Press: 2000), 83.

75. Ibid., 146.

76. James Gorman, "Bird Lovers Hope to Keep Cats on a Very Short Leash," *New York Times* (18 March 2003).

77. Susan Hodara, "Caretakers of Cats Make It Official," *New York Times: Westchester section* (6 April 2003).

78. Elsa Wolfson, "How to Help Homeless Cats," *CatWatch*, a publication of the Cornell University College of Veterinary Medicine (March 2003), 8.

79. Karen Lee Stevens, "'Holidays' to Help Cats," *CatWatch*, a publication of the Cornell University College of Veterinary Medicine (April 2003), 4.

80. Peter B. Churcher and John H. Lawton, "Predation by Domestic Cats in an English Village," *Journal of Zoology, London*, a publication of the Zoological Society of London (1987), 439–455.

81. Peter B. Churcher and John H. Lawton, "Beware of Well-Fed Felines: Britain's Five Million House Cats Enjoy Both Indoor Comforts and Outdoor Hunting," *Natural History* (July 1989), 47.

82. Leon Jaroff, "Attack of the Killer Cats: A Study Shows That Those Lovable Furry Pets Decimate Wildlife," *Time* (31 July 1989).

83. Roger Tabor, *Cats: The Rise of the Cat* (London: BBC Books, 1991), 85.

84. One of the earliest researchers to investigate the diets of free-roaming cats, Paul L. Errington, states this succinctly in 1936, in his "Notes on Food Habits of Southern Wisconsin House Cats" *Journal of Mammalogy* 17:1 (1936), 65. "Preying upon a species is not necessarily synonymous with controlling it, or even influencing its numbers to any perceptible degree. Predation which merely removes an exposed prey surplus that is naturally doomed anyway is entirely different from predation the weight of which is instrumental in forcing down prey populations or in holding them at given approximate levels."

85. B. Mike Fitzgerald and Dennis C. Turner, "Hunting Behaviour of Domestic Cats and Their Impact on Prey Populations," in *The Domestic Cat: The Biology of Its Behaviour, 2nd edition,* ed. by Dennis C. Turner and Patrick Bateson (Cambridge: Cambridge University Press, 2000), 151–175. This chapter, with almost four pages of references, can be considered the ultimate resource on the subject of cat predation throughout the world.

86. "What the Cat Dragged In," *Catnip*, a publication of the Tufts University School of Veterinary Medicine 2:12 (1995), 4–6.

87. "Cats Indoors! The Campaign for Safer Birds and Cats," American Bird Conservancy (24 September 1997), 6.

88. Ellen Perry Berkeley, "On Predation," in *Maverick Cats,* op. cit., 66–75. Birds made up only 4 percent of the cats' diet (by volume) in an Oklahoma study in 1941; only 5.2 percent (by volume) in an Australian study in 1972; and only 4.5 percent (by weight) in a New Zealand study in 1979.

89. B. M. Fitzgerald, "Diet of Domestic Cats and Their Impact on Prey Populations," in *The Domestic Cat: The Biology of Its Behaviour,* ed. by Dennis C. Turner and Patrick Bateson (Cambridge: Cambridge University Press, 1988), 123–147.

90. John S. Coleman and Stanley A. Temple, "How Many Birds Do Cats Kill?" (University of Wisconsin Department of Wildlife Ecology, 24 February 1994), 2 pages. *See also* John S. Coleman and Stanley A. Temple, "On the Prowl: In Suburban Backyards and Rural Fields, Free-roaming Cats Are Pouncing on Songbird Populations," *Wisconsin Natural Resources* 20 (December 1996), 4–8. *See also* John S. Coleman, Stanley A. Temple, and Scott R. Craven, "Cats and Wildlife: A Conservation Dilemma" (University of Wisconsin-Extension, 1997), 6 pages.

91. Linda Winter, letter to Ellen Perry Berkeley, 10 November 1998.

92. John S. Coleman and Stanley A. Temple, "How Many Birds Do Cats Kill?" op. cit.

93. B. M. Fitzgerald, letter to Ellen Perry Berkeley, 28 September 1998.

94. B. Mike Fitzgerald and Dennis C. Turner, "Hunting Behaviour of Domestic Cats and Their Impact on Prey Populations," in *The Domestic Cat: The Biology of Its Behaviour, 2nd edition,* op. cit., 164–166. The continental studies that Fitzgerald included are from the northern hemisphere (Europe and North America combined) and from Australia. The island studies he included are from two kinds of islands: those with landbirds but *without seabirds*

recorded in the diet (various sites in New Zealand, the Canary Islands, Hawaii, Socorro, and Christmas Island), and those *with seabirds* recorded in the diet (subantarctic islands such as Marion, Kerguelen, and Campbell, and a few tropical islands).

95. B. M. Fitzgerald, letter to Ellen Perry Berkeley, 12 October 1999.

96. Ibid.

97. "Keeping Cats Indoors Isn't Just for the Birds," American Bird Conservancy, 1998, 8 pages.

98. "Domestic Cat Predation on Birds and Other Wildlife," website of the American Bird Conservancy (www.abcbirds.org), downloaded 18 September 2003, 4 pages.

99. Merritt Clifton, "Where Cats Belong—and Where They Don't," op. cit., 17.

100. *State of the World 2003: A Worldwatch Institute Report on Progress Toward a Sustainable Society* (New York: W. W. Norton & Company, 2003), 16.

101. Merritt Clifton, "Where Cats Belong—and Where They Don't," op. cit., 17.

102. Ibid., 17.

103. Paul Leyhausen, *Cat Behavior: The Predatory and Social Behavior of Domestic and Wild Cats* (New York: Garland STPM Press, 1979), 78. Even in such circumstances—where the cats are forced to concentrate their energies on songbirds—Leyhausen concludes that the cats are "not capable of seriously endangering the songbird population of a substantial area."

104. "Splenetic Considerations," *Cats & Kittens* (November 2000), 9.

105. Kevin R. Crooks and Michael E. Soulé, "Mesopredator Release and Avifaunal Extinctions in a Fragmented System," *Nature* (August 1999), 563–566. The "mesopredator release hypothesis," which these researchers admit "remains controversial," is described by them in this way: "Mammalian carnivores are particularly vulnerable to extinction in fragmented landscapes, and their disappearance may lead to increased numbers of smaller carnivores that are principle [sic] predators of birds and other small vertebrates." In coastal southern California (an area "fragmented by development"), the canyons stand out as "habitat islands in an urban sea." The most common large predator—the coyote—has declined in these canyons, leading to increased numbers of mesopredators: the striped skunk, raccoon, grey fox, domestic cat, and opossum. And, in the process, state these researchers, scrub-breeding birds have suffered. A critical reading of the article,

however, reveals statements that mesopredator pressure, together with other fragmentation effects, "may" drive native prey species to extinction, and that at least 75 local extinctions "may have occurred" in these fragments over the past century. We might well wonder whether the domestic cat is the major contributor to this situation that "may" be occurring (as the American Bird Conservancy might wish us to believe, quoting figures that make Crooks and Soulé look like Churcher and Lawton). And we might well want to remind opponents of TNR that only TNR can *reduce* the feral cat population in an area over the long run. Still, though, this article suggests to even the most ardent TNR advocate that such a landscape might not be the best place for TNR, at least in part because the few coyotes in the area would be interested in hunting the cats. The world is a complicated place.

106. Among these places is Cape May, NJ. "This is the birding capital of the United States; we're right in the middle of the Eastern flyway," says John Queenan, head of animal control for Cape May and a leading advocate of TNR. His successful TNR program, currently under attack by the National Audubon Society, has been in place in Cape May since 1995. Audubon alleges that the piping plover is under threat from these feral cats, but Queenan replies that the Audubon case is based on a Wisconsin projection that is seriously questioned even for that state. Queenan tells me (in a telephone interview, 19 February 2004) that foxes, raccoons, dogs, and even owned cats go after the piping plover more than these managed feral cats do. Another place where TNR is being charged with damaging native species is Key Largo, FL, where a successful TNR program at Ocean Reef is supported by the following: 1) primarily by the nonprofit ORCAT organization, which pays for all ongoing expenses such as veterinary fees, medical supplies, cat food, etc.; 2) secondarily by the community association (provider of various services to the community), which pays for the salaries of the three ORCAT employees; and 3) lastly by the local club (owner of the local hotel and composed of members and homeowners), which donates clinic space and golf-cart transportation. Here, on Key Largo, the allegation is that TNR has damaged the cotton mouse and wood rat, but Susan Hershey of ORCAT tells me (in a telephone interview, 17 February 2004) that there is "no scientific evidence of their decline." And, she adds, "the community loves this program—even the people who don't love cats, love it," because a population of about 2,500 feral cats almost a decade ago has been reduced to about 500, under the managed care of TNR. (For additional places where TNR has had no negative effect on endangered species, contact Alley Cat Allies.)

107. "Keeping Cats Indoors Isn't Just for the Birds," op. cit.

108. " 'Managed' Cat Colonies: The Wrong Solution to a Tragic Problem," American Bird Conservancy website, downloaded 18 September 2003, 3 pages.

109. This new "Glossary of Feral Cat Terms" appears on the new website of "Wild About Cats!" (www.wild-about-cats.com). "Wild About Cats!" is a comprehensive educational campaign inaugurated on National Feral Cat Day, 16 October 2003, and sponsored jointly by Alley Cat Allies and Best Friends Animal Society, "to promote an understanding of the feral cat's nature, origins, history, social structure, and niche in our society and environment. . . . No spin, no extrapolation, no misinformation." The "Glossary of Feral Cat Terms" also appeared in the Winter 2003 issue of *Feral Cat Activist*, a publication of Alley Cat Allies.

110. "Wildlife Policy Statement: Feral and Free-Ranging Domestic Cats," (The Wildlife Society, 24 September 2002), 2 pages. This item about the humane elimination of feral cat colonies is first in the statement's series of 10 items.

111. "Draft Position Statement: Feral and Free-Ranging Domestic Cats," (The Wildlife Society, 2000), 1 page. As in 2002, this item is first in the 2000 statement. But the earlier statement, interestingly, has the following policy, dropped in 2002: to "encourage the management of native predators in wildlands, especially in the urban wildland interface, where they could provide a natural check on free-ranging domestic cats."

112. "Wildlife Policy Statement: Feral and Free-Ranging Domestic Cats," (2002), op. cit.

113. Doris Day Animal League website (www.ddal.org), downloaded 2 April 2003.

114. *Best Friends for Life: Humane Housing for Animals and People* (Doris Day Animal League and Massachusetts Society for the Prevention of Cruelty to Animals, 2001), 50 pages. (One copy is available free, from the website of the Doris Day Animal League (www.ddal.org) or by telephoning DDAL at 202-546-1761.

115. Ibid., 36–37.

116. Kat Burns (manager, donor and member services), telephone interview with Ellen Perry Berkeley, 24 March 2003.

117. "Feral Cats Policy Statement," Animal Protection Services of the

American Humane Association (1998), 1 page.

118. "A More Humane Approach to Feral Cat Population Management," 2 pages, website of Best Friends Animal Society (www.bestfriends.org), downloaded 3 August 2003.

119. "A Safe Cat Is a Happy Cat," The Humane Society of the United States (2002), 5.

120. Margaret R. Slater, *Community Approaches to Feral Cats: Problems, Alternatives & Recommendations* (Washington, DC: Humane Society Press, an affiliate of The Humane Society of the United States 2002), 3, 13, 87. This 140-page book is available from HSUS, 2100 L Street NW, Washington, DC 20037 for $22.50 plus $3 shipping. A PDF version of the book is available for download, free, on the website of HSUS (www.hsus.org).

121. Susan Hagood, "Cats and Wildlife: Motivate the Public with a Pro-Cat Message," *Wildlife Tracks*, a publication of The Humane Society of the United States (Spring 2000), 1, 3–5, 16.

122. Ibid., 4.

123. "Pros, Cons of Feral and Free-Ranging Cat Management Debated: Biologists Warn about Environmental, Legal, and Ethical Implications," *AVMA Convention Daily News* (16 July 2003).

124. Sandra Sebastian, telephone interview with Ellen Perry Berkeley, 25 March 2003.

125. Marion S. Lane, "January Cats," *Animal Watch*, a publication of the American Society for the Prevention of Cruelty to Animals (Spring 2003), 2.

126. Paul A. Rees, "The Ecology and Management of Feral Cat Colonies," Ph.D. thesis, University of Bradford, England, 1982, 469 pages.

127. Paul A. Rees, "The Ecological Distribution of Feral Cats and the Effects of Neutering a Hospital Colony," in *The Ecology and Control of Feral Cats*, op. cit., 22.

128. Peter F. Neville and Jenny Remfry, "Effect of Neutering on Two Groups of Feral Cats," op. cit. *See also* Peter F. Neville, "Humane Control of an Urban Cat Colony," op. cit.

129. Peter F. Neville, "Humane Control of an Urban Cat Colony," op. cit. Between the two methods—continually destroying the constantly increasing number of feral cats living in the basement garage of a large housing estate,

or keeping the colony at a manageable level by neutering the cats—an estimate of the cost differential over a 10-year period is startling: £4,000 for the former method; £1,700 for the latter.

130. Roger Tabor, *The Wild Life of the Domestic Cat* (London: Arrow Books, 1982), 223 pages. This book is often erroneously listed as *The* Wildlife *of the Domestic Cat*—even, outrageously, on the cover of Tabor's own book. Biographical notes in all his later publications correct this error.

131. Roger Tabor, *The Wild Life of the Domestic Cat*, op. cit., 182. *See also* Roger Tabor, *Understanding Cats* (Devon: David & Charles, 1995), 42.

132. Warner C. Passanisi and David W. Macdonald, *The Fate of Controlled Feral Cat Colonies*, op. cit.

133. Ibid., 5, 42.

134. Ibid., 42.

135. Ibid., 43–44.

136. Karl I. Zaunbrecher and Richard E. Smith, "Neutering of Feral Cats as an Alternative to Eradication Programs," *Journal of the American Veterinary Medical Association* 203:3 (1 August 1993), 449–452. In the years since 1993, word has spread that these two researchers had retracted their support of TNR. Not so. In several telephone conversations I had with Dr. Zaunbrecher on 2 February and 11 February 2004, he said unequivocally to me, "I stand by that work. It's the pilot program. Everybody follows it." About TNR in general, he said to me, "I'm very much in favor of TNR. Eradication is a complete failure everywhere. Eradication won't make the problem go away; it only makes the problem worse." But then come some ambiguities. Zaunbrecher believes that the natural environment will support only a small number of feral cats—which will be news to scientists who have studied feral cats living in substantial numbers in relatively (or wholly) uninhabited places. Further, Zaunbrecher believes, "If you want to get rid of the difficulties caused by large concentrations of feral cats around a food source, you have to stop feeding them," as he said to me. Thus there are situations for Zaunbrecher where it would seem appropriate to do other than TNR. I pressed him for an example, and he replied that if, for instance, the cats were living in a dangerous place for them, he would envision "closing off that ecological niche by not feeding the cats, at the same time removing the cats." This is perhaps what has been interpreted as his fully favoring "eradication" over TNR, but I think instead that his stance is quite other—he favors TNR, almost fully, over eradication. He has not published anything on TNR since

1993 and does not consider himself an authority on feral cats, thinking of himself as simply a "country doctor"—he is a veterinarian practicing in upstate New York. His mentor, Dr. Smith, is now deceased. Prior to the 1993 research, Smith had done a similar project, the results of which were never published, says Zaunbrecher.

137. Ibid., 452.

138. Ibid., 452.

139. R. Lee Zasloff and Lynette A. Hart, "Attitudes and Care Practices of Cat Caretakers in Hawaii, *Anthrozoös,* a publication of the Delta Society, 11:4 (1998), 242–248.

140. Ibid., 242.

141. Irene T. Lee, Julie K. Levy, Shawn P. Gorman, P. Cynda Crawford, and Margaret R. Slater, "Prevalence of Feline Leukemia Virus Infection and Serum Antibodies against Feline Immunodeficiency Virus in Unowned Free-Roaming Cats," *Journal of the American Veterinary Medical Association* 220:5 (1 March 2002), 620–622.

142. Ibid., 620. The totals for each of the two areas—Raleigh, NC, and Gainesville, FL—were similar. For the 733 unowned free-roaming cats tested in the Raleigh area, the overall prevalence of FeLV infection was 5.3 percent; the overall seroprevalence for FIV was 2.3 percent. For the 1,143 unowned free-roaming cats tested in the Gainesville area, the figures were 4.3 percent and 3.5 percent respectively. Such low figures compare favorably with these viruses in *pet* cats, as shown in a 1989 Seattle study cited by Lee, Levy, et al. The Seattle study showed 7 percent for FeLV and 4 percent for FIV among the pet cats. I noticed, however, that Lee, Levy, et al., make no mention of two other papers giving quite different results. In the first of these, "Parasite Prevalence in Free-Ranging Farm Cats, Felis silvestris catus," by Yamaguchi, et al., published in 1996 in England, no animals at all in the test population of "50–80 feral cats" (at a farm in Oxfordshire) tested positive for FeLV, while antibodies for FIV were found in a very high 53 percent. A second paper, by Courchamp and Pontier, "Feline Immunodeficiency Virus: An Epidemiological Review," published in 1994 in France, is cited by Yamaguchi, et al., as concluding that "Worldwide, feral cats have an FIV infection rate of 16%, compared with only 5% for cats kept indoors, and 12% for household cats with outdoor access." I asked Dr. Levy about these two papers. Regarding the Yamaguchi paper, which she rightly identifies as the study of "a small group of cats from a small area," she points to its "unusual pattern

of infections"—no FeLV cats, and no correlation between the FIV cats and the classic risk factors. She therefore considers this study an "outlier" (an "exception") that "should not be extrapolated to other situations or larger populations." Regarding the Courchamp paper, which she rightly identifies as "a review of many other papers," she comments that "Since many of the papers tested only 'high risk' or sick cats, the rate of FIV is falsely elevated if extrapolated to the population of all cats." (Julie K. Levy, letter to Ellen Perry Berkeley, 11 December 2003.)

143. Lindsay S. Williams, Julie K. Levy, Sheilah A. Robertson, Alexis M. Cistola, and Lisa A. Centonze, "Use of the Anesthetic Combination of Tiletamine, Zolazepam, Ketamine, and Xylazine for Neutering Feral Cats," *Journal of the American Veterinary Medical Association* 220:10 (15 May 2002, 1491–1495.

144. Ibid., 1494.

145. Ibid., 1494.

146. Ibid., 1494.

147. Lisa A. Centonze and Julie K. Levy, "Characteristics of Free-Roaming Cats and Their Caretakers," *Journal of the American Veterinary Medical Association* 220:11 (1 June 2002), 1627–1633.

148. Ibid., 1632.

149. Ibid., 1627.

150. Ibid., 1633.

151. Karen C. Scott, Julie K. Levy, and P. Cynda Crawford, "Characteristics of Free-Roaming Cats Evaluated in a Trap-Neuter-Return Program," *Journal of the American Veterinary Medical Association* 221:8 (15 October 2002), 1136–1138.

152. Ibid., 1136.

153. Ibid., 1136.

154. Julie K. Levy, David W. Gale, and Leslie A. Gale, "Evaluation of the Effect of a Long-Term Trap-Neuter-Return and Adoption Program on a Free-Roaming Cat Population," *Journal of the American Veterinary Medical Association*, 222:1 (1 January 2003), 42–46.

155. Ibid., 45.

156. Ibid., 46.

157. Daniel Castillo, "Population Estimates and Behavioral Analyses of Managed Cat (*Felis catus*) Colonies Located in Miami-Dade County, Florida, Parks," a thesis for the degree of M.S. in environmental studies, Florida International University (2001), 61 pages.

158. Ibid., iv, 42.

159. Ibid., 23, 29, 30. "Dumping" is a particularly complex issue. People who become aware of a well-run TNR program will often abandon an unwanted pet at that location, expecting that the cat will be properly cared for by those already caring for the existing colony. (Expecting that the dumped cat will be welcomed into that feral colony is another matter—not always the case.) Some abandoned cats adapt quickly to feral life, but others have great difficulty learning to survive outdoors. Often the newly strayed cat will look dirty and disheveled, fitting right in with the common image of a feral cat, while the feral cat will look clean and sleek because it's not spending all its time trying to learn how to survive. The transition from lost or abandoned cat to successful outdoor survivor is eased if the cat is lucky enough to be accepted into a feral colony, especially into a managed colony where the caretaker is always on the lookout for—and always ready to receive—another creature in need. Proper management of a TNR colony, therefore, must include continual monitoring—knowing the members of the group, identifying them by the trimmed ear, and checking them regularly for health problems. Of critical importance, too, proper management must recognize newcomers. Every newcomer must be trapped, then sterilized, vaccinated, and eartipped before being returned to the colony. This requirement is spelled out in every guide that explains TNR's goals and procedures. Unfortunately, dumping is also mentioned by every opponent of TNR. But dumping need not be a reason to oppose TNR; instead, dumping can be considered just one more piece of the problem. The solution is readily available—it is the same Trap-Neuter-Return that has already been undertaken for long-term members of the colony. The larger solution—building a cat-owning consciousness that precludes abandonment—is also within reach, and being worked on throughout the humane movement.

160. Cindy Hewitt (executive director, Cat Network), letters to Ellen Perry Berkeley, 11 and 14 December 2003. Even newspaper stories about adoption possibilities would bring dumping, says a former coordinator of the TNR work at Crandon. (Kate Rhubee letter to Ellen Perry Berkeley, 20 February 2004) By the time Rhubee had left Key Biscayne, she was starting to see

dumped cats with tipped ears. She attributes this to a Cat Network member thinking that the cats would be better off at the marina than on the streets. But Rhubee was never able to catch the person doing it, and "of course no one ever confessed." All of this suggests that Castillo might well have done his research at a more typical TNR site, or might at least have mentioned these factors in his research report.

161. Lynn MacAuley, "TNR—Myth or Fact: An Analysis of the Issues," unpublished (2003), 24 pages.

162. Ibid., 7.

163. Ibid., 7.

164. Julie Levy, letter to Ellen Perry Berkeley, 23 June 2003.

165. Ibid.

166. Kimberly B. Subacz, "Assessing the Impact of Trap-Neuter-Return on the Management of Feral Cats," forthcoming M.S. thesis in wildlife, Auburn University.

167. Kimberly B. Subacz, "Assessing the Impact of Trap-Neuter-Return on the Management of Feral Cats: Project Description" (undated), sent to Ellen Perry Berkeley, 20 March 2003, 2.

168. Lynn Spivak (director of communications, Maddie's Fund), letter to Ellen Perry Berkeley, 30 January 2004. Tracking is of critical importance to the continued growth of the TNR movement. Without tracking, states Becky Robinson of Alley Cat Allies, we do not know where the cats came from, whether they were in managed colonies, how many cats were at those locations at the start and end of the program, how many complaints about the cats (offensive behaviors, sickly animals, endless litters, etc.) were received before and after the program, and what the status of the cats' health and care was before and after. Without such tracking, Robinson continues, we cannot know whether the neutering effort has made any real dent in the overall feral cat population. Because only comprehensive and communitywide programs can substantially reduce the number of feral cats (small-scale and scattered efforts cannot), says Robinson, the need at present is for "accurate statistics from well-run programs" as "the only way to convince elected officials, animal control officers, and other policy makers that TNR will get results." Fortunately, TNR advocates are increasingly turning their energies and professional skills toward these efforts. The Animal Coalition of Tampa (in Hillsborough County, FL) is one such group. Headed by Frank and Linda

Hamilton, it focuses its efforts on the neighborhoods that produce the most complaints about feral cats, working with animal control to find out which neighborhoods those are and keeping detailed records of all pertinent data. Feral Friends (in the Dallas/Fort Worth Metroplex) is another such group. Headed by Susan Kilgore, and starting its TNR work as recently as 2002, Feral Friends uses current maps and long-term projections to document its progress. As Becky Robinson sums it up, "I consider the programs that the Hamiltons, Susan Kilgore, and others like them have developed to be the 'present' of TNR. The 'future' is when animal control agencies universally accept nonlethal population control methods as the standard. We will get to the future by expanding upon the work that Frank and Susan, et al., are doing today."

169. Lynn Spivak, telephone interview with Ellen Perry Berkeley, 25 March 2003.

170. Richard Avanzino, "Maddie's Fund: How can my community get money from Maddie's Fund?" 3–7 March 2003, on No More Homeless Pets Forum (www.bestfriends.org).

171. Lynn Spivak, letter to Ellen Perry Berkeley, 30 January 2004.

172. "The Feral Fix," on the website of No More Homeless Pets in Utah, a program of Best Friends Animal Sanctuary, now Best Friends Animal Society, www.utahpets.org, downloaded 6 June 2003.

173. "Feral Cat Colony Registration System Launched in NYC" (20 September 2002), on the Neighborhood Cats website (www.neighborhoodcats.org), downloaded 7 April 2003.

174. "Summary of Program Costs vs Incoming Cats—Humane Society of Santa Clara Valley and the Cities of San Jose, Milpitas, Santa Clara, Campbell, Cupertino, Los Gatos, Monte Sereno, Saratoga, and Sunnyvale," 2 pages, National Pet Alliance website (www.nationalpetalliance.com), linking to the National Pet Alliance and its Study Reports, downloaded 3 December 2003. Additional information from telephone interview with Karen Johnson (a founder, now a director of the National Pet Alliance), 3 December 2003.

175. Brenda Griffin, summary statement accompanying *Proceedings of the 2002 Symposium on Nonsurgical Methods for Pet Population Control* (undated), 1 page. The full *Proceedings*, which run to 118 pages in hard copy, can be obtained from the website of the Alliance for Contraception in Cats and Dogs (www.vetmed.vt.edu/accd).

176. "Introducing a Different Needle," *Animal People* (September 2000), 3. This estimate followed an important gathering of immunosterilant researchers in July 2000, brought together by Esther Mechler's SPAY/USA. Reporting on this conference, Merritt Clifton mentions the researchers' general agreement that "broad use of immunosterilants in dogs and cats is 'two to five years away,'" but that the researchers linked their estimate to the success of current experiments and to the additional work needed to get governmental approval. This last is an important reservation. We see that Neutersol®, the puppy-neutering drug that was approved in 2003, took 12 years (!) to get Food and Drug Administration approval; the approval process began in 1991, reported *Paws to Think*, a publication of The Pet Savers Foundation, in its Summer 2003 issue (p. 10). I was so stunned by this length of time that—suspecting a typographical error—I checked with Dr. Brenda Griffin, one of the outstanding researchers in this field. "1991, yes that is correct," she replied to me; "the process is long, but need not be that long."

177. Robert T. Perry, "More on Finding Funding," in *Proceedings of the 2002 Symposium on Nonsurgical Methods for Pet Population Control,* op. cit., 81.

178. Linda Rhodes, "The Pharmaceutical Industry's Role in Development, Registration and Production of a Contraceptive for Dogs and Cats," in *Proceedings of the 2002 Symposium on Nonsurgical Methods for Pet Population Control,* op. cit., 89.

179. Stephen M. Boyle, letter to Ellen Perry Berkeley, 20 March 2003. Still, Boyle is quoted in an article by Sally Deneen, "Birth Control for Cats," in *Catnip,* a publication of the Tufts University School of Veterinary Medicine (November 2003), 10–12, as believing that an oral vaccine for cats is "realistically, several years away from being available." It is truly anybody's guess.

180. Henry J. Baker, summary of "Regulation, Funding and Marketing of Contraceptive Products" session, accompanying *Proceedings of the 2002 Symposium on Nonsurgical Methods for Pet Population Control* (undated), 2 pages.

181. "Finding Funding," in *Proceedings of the 2002 Symposium on Nonsurgical Methods for Pet Population Control,* op. cit., 79.

182. Brenda Griffin, summary of "Pet Overpopulation and Strategies for Control" session, accompanying *Proceedings of the 2002 Symposium on Nonsurgical Methods for Pet Population Control* (undated) 2 pages.

183. For full information on the extent of TNR practiced across America, check with Alley Cat Allies. Its "Feral Friends Network" alone will speak

volumes. Additional information is available from Alley Cat Allies on a wide variety of subjects—on the latest political battles regarding TNR, on model TNR programs around the country, on cold-weather protection for managed colonies, on a do-it-yourself cat fence, on eartipping, on trap selection, on safe relocation of feral cats, on fundraising—and much more.

184. "Latest U.S. Data Shows Shelter Killing Down to 4.2 Million/Year," *Animal People* (July/August 2003), 17.

185. "San Francisco Posts New Records for Saving Homeless Cats and Dogs," on the website of the SF/SPCA (www.sfspca.org), downloaded 20 March 2003.

186. Deanna Mather Larson, "The Feral Cat Fix (A *Cats & Kittens* Special Report)" *Cats & Kittens* (July 2003), 21–22.

187. "What Does the FCCO Do?" from the website of the Feral Cat Coalition of Oregon (www.feralcats.com), downloaded 23 May 2003. There's some indication, however, that mobile clinics may not be the wave of the future. In *Animal People* (October 2003), 4, replying to a letter to the editor, Merritt Clifton wrote that "many pioneers of the approach are rethinking it." He cited several examples of this rethinking, which holds that bringing a mobile surgical clinic to the cats is both more costly and less efficient than bringing the cats to a fixed location for surgery. For the utmost efficiency, one vet now uses his mobile unit not for surgeries but to carry supplies and to bring all elements of a portable hospital that he can set up "within minutes." He has found that "resupply is often a bigger problem than finding a place to improvise a surgical theatre."

188. Information from TEAM's ads, brochures, and website (www.everyanimalmatters.org/feline.html), downloaded 1 July 2003.

189. "Feral Cat Sterilization Now Available Throughout Alachua County," e-mail from Julie Levy to Ellen Perry Berkeley, 1 March 2003, 2 pages.

190. Linda Kelson, "The Race to Outpace Feral Cat Over-Population" (1998), on the website of the Feral Cat Coalition (www.feralcat.com), downloaded 3 April 2003.

191. Nathan J. Winograd, letter to Ellen Perry Berkeley, 25 March 2003.

192. Nathan J. Winograd, "Going No-Kill: No-kill overnight? Can't be." on No More Homeless Pets Forum, 17–21 February 2003 (www.bestfriends.org).

193. Denise Eufusia (chair of the Board of Directors, Forgotten Felines of Sonoma County) telephone interview with Ellen Perry Berkeley, 20 August 2003.

194. Abbie Wolf (project manager of ASPCA's National Shelter Outreach), telephone interview with Ellen Perry Berkeley, 2 December 2003.

195. Joyce Briggs (associate executive director, PETsMART Charities), telephone interview with, and letter to, Ellen Perry Berkeley, 24–25 November 2003.

196. Robert T. Perry (director, Environment and Welfare of Animals, Geraldine R. Dodge Foundation), letter to Ellen Perry Berkeley, 4 December 2003.

197. Kathy L. Hughes, Margaret R. Slater, and Linda Haller, "The Effects of Implementing a Feral Cat Spay/Neuter Program in a Florida County Animal Control Service," *Journal of Applied Animal Welfare Science*, 5:4 (2002), 285–298. From the article: "The average cost per surgery was $56. The average total cost per impounded animal for impounding, shelter, and processing the complaint was $139. For the 7,903 feral cats neutered, the cost was an estimated $442,568. The estimated cost, if these cats were impounded and euthanized, was $1,098,517, a difference of $655,949."

198. Karen Johnson, "San Jose Fixing Ferals," letter to the editor, *Animal People* (June 1995), 4; also "Fixing the Problem in San Jose," letter to the editor, *Animal People* (June 1998), 4.

199. "Where Does TNR Work?" Alley Cat Allies, 2002. This 1-page list (described by ACA as "far from complete") is intended to show the "scope and breadth" of TNR in the United States and Canada. The list gives 7 examples of public/private funding, 8 examples of public funding, and 32 examples of private funding—all of which, impressive enough for their "scope and breadth," are only a sample of the extensive TNR work done throughout the United States and Canada.

200. "Laws That Have Passed," *Spay/Neuter Legislation Bulletin*, a publication of The Fund for Animals (March 1996), 1.

201. Janet Scarlett, telephone interview with Ellen Perry Berkeley, 28 April 2003.

202. "From Animal Control to Animal Care: One County Shows How It's Done," *Best Friends Magazine*, a publication of Best Friends Animal Sanctuary, now Best Friends Animal Society (January/February 2003), 15, 16. *See also* Ed Boks, "Working With Animal Control: What is the role of animal control?" on No More Homeless Pets Forum, 6–10 January 2003 (www.bestfriends.org).

203. The 70 percent figure comes from Merritt Clifton, "Street Dog and Feral

Cat Sterilization and Vaccination Efforts Must Get 70% or Flunk," *Animal People* (October 2002), 1, 6–7. Replying to a letter to the editor in *Animal People* (December 2002), 4, Clifton mentions this figure as coming from the work of Leonardo Fibonacci of Pisa, born in 1170, who was studying agricultural productivity. Six centuries later, writes Clifton, this work furnished Pasteur's 70 percent target for vaccination effectiveness. The 88 percent figure, on the other hand, comes from the website of the Alliance for Contraception in Cats and Dogs (www.vetmed.vt.edu/accd), which opens a page with this intriguing message: "A study in one mid-western state suggested that 88% of all feral cats would have to be spayed to maintain zero population growth." Checking further with Dr. Stephen Boyle, I learned that this study of population dynamics was done by researchers R. Nassar and J. E. Mosier. Their results were published in the article "Feline Population Dynamics: A Study of the Manhattan, Kansas, Feline Population," *American Journal of Veterinary Research* (1982, 43:1), 167–170. Another person who has written in support of a high level of sterilization done quickly within a circumscribed area is Dr. W. Marvin Mackie, the owner/director of two Animal Birth Control clinics in Los Angeles, and a veterinarian nationally recognized for his work in early-age sterilization. Supporting "the 70 percent rule" himself, Mackie cites its support also by epidemiologists, and by public health authorities such as the World Health Organization and the Centers for Disease Control. In his article "Pet Overpopulation and the 70% Rule"—reprinted in *Paws to Think*, a publication of The Pet Savers Foundation (Winter 2004), 16–17—Mackie writes that massive pet sterilization must occur within a short period of time and within a well-defined area. Thus, while a mobile spay/neuter unit traveling to outlying areas one day every month may be "good for public relations," it "cannot achieve the number of sterilizations required in any one area to significantly reduce over-birthing." (An area, as defined by Mackie, can be anything from an isolated town or community to "the mere acreage of a feral cat colony.")

204. On the UFAW website (www.ufaw.org.uk), for instance, one can order *Feral Cats: Suggestions for Control* (1995), the 19-page 3rd edition of this ground-breaking guide, for $7. (For those not yet on the Internet, write to UFAW at The Old School, Brewhouse Hill, Wheathampstead, Hertfordshire AL4 8AN, U.K.) On the "Marketplace" pages of the ACA website (www.alleycat.org/books.html), in addition to materials produced by ACA, one can find Susan Easterly's book, *The Guide to Handraising Kittens*, for $8; Operation Catnip's *Idealism in Action*, a 195-page guide to running a high-volume spay/neuter clinic for feral cats, for $12; Tamara Kreuz's book, *The Stray Cat Handbook*, telling how to care for stray and feral cats, for $10—and much more.

205. Among the newest books with a segment on TNR is *Living in Shadows: How to Help the Stray Cat in Your Life (without adding to the problem)*, by Ann K. Fisher (Los Angeles: Amythyst Publishing, 2002).

206. *9 Lives: Humane Feral Cats Management* includes the following nine tapes: humane trapping of feral cats, handling and treating feral cats, care and feeding of feral cats, caring for newborn kittens, nonlethal feral cat programs, relocating feral cats, feral cat advocacy, socializing feral cats, and successful programs at work. Tapes are $9.95 each; $79.95 for the set. Order from SF/SPCA, 2500 16th Street, San Francisco, CA 94103, or www.sfspca.org.

207. ACA's *Trap-Neuter-Return: A Humane Approach to Feral Cat Control* (a comprehensive training video "for novices and pros alike") is 24 minutes in length. ACA's *The Humane Solution: Reducing Feral Cat Populations with Trap-Neuter-Return* (a persuasive video for decision-makers) is 9:56 minutes in length. Each tape is $13; together they are $20.

208. FCC's tape covers talking to the public, planning clinics, coordinating volunteers, doing effective trapping, lending out traps, detailing clinic procedures, providing medical care—and more. Send $15 to FCC at PMB 160, 9528 Miramar Rd., San Diego, CA 92126.

209. To purchase *Working with Feral Cats in Veterinary Practice*, contact Dr. Larry Moore, Biomedical Communications, College of Veterinary Medicine, Auburn University, AL 36849 (telephone: 334-844-4095). Price is $15 for the video, $25 for the DVD (postage within the United States is included).

210. From its ad, this course covers "all aspects of responsible colony management, including building good community relations, feeding, shelter, trapping, and spay/neuter. Choose quick download ($14.95) or discussion board ($19.95)." Find the course on www.neighborhoodcats.org and click on "Study TNR Online."

211. "Campus Cats," *Alley Cat Action*, a publication of Alley Cat Allies (Fall 1999), 3. An early aim of this group was to neuter all feral cats on campus and, thus, between 1986 and 1989, some 250 cats were sterilized by senior students, under the guidance of faculty members. Julie Levy was then a veterinary student at that institution; one of her noteworthy studies there (with two of her professors) was a comparison of 80 feral cats and 70 pet cats, a study showing virtually the same rate of infection of FeLV and FIV for each population.

212. Stanford Cat Network website, www.stanford.edu/group/CATNET, downloaded 4 April 2003.

213. Lucy V. Evans, "Campus Crusade: A University-Based SPCA," *Animal Watch*, a publication of ASPCA (Summer 2003), 53.

214. UT Campus Cat Coalition website (www.ae.utexas.edu/cats), downloaded 11 November 2003.

215. Most of these campus-based TNR programs are given as links on the UT Campus Cat Coalition website (www.ae.utexas.edu/cats), downloaded 11 November 2003.

216. Brenda Griffin, Kelly Hume, Jodi Howell, Kim Smith, Robert Parsley, Rusty Morton, Cathy Parsley, and Kim Klopfenstein, "Progress of Operation Cat Nap in Controlling the Feral Cat Population on the Auburn University Campus," in *Proceedings of the 2002 Symposium on Nonsurgical Methods for Pet Population Control*, op. cit., 104.

217. "Vets for Life: Ensuring the Future of Trap-Neuter-Return," *Alley Cat Action*, a publication of Alley Cat Allies (Summer 2002), 1, 2. At the time, notes ACA, "fewer than five of the more than 27 schools for veterinary medicine and schools for veterinary technicians in the United States teach students how to treat feral cats."

218. "Calling All Vets: Why They're Working Closely with Rescue Groups," *Best Friends Magazine*, a publication of Best Friends Animal Sanctuary, now Best Friends Animal Society (March/April 2003), 19.

219. "Feral Cats 101," *Best Friends Magazine*, a publication of Best Friends Animal Sanctuary, now Best Friends Animal Society (November/December 2001), 32.

220. *Annual Review*, The Cats Protection League (1993), 7. See also *Annual Review*, The Cats Protection League (1995), 4, for the growth of this policy. By 1995, in fact, 10 percent of all cats helped by the league were feral. Today, Cats Protection distributes a letter in which Cats Protection offers financial assistance in the neutering of any "reasonable sized colony" of feral cats, so long as the "ongoing welfare" of the cats is assured, either at their original location or at "a suitable alternative site." (This financial assistance, emphasizes Cats Protection, is for neutering costs only, not for costs of treatment or euthanasia). Today, too, Cats Protection has a four-page brochure, published in 1999, entitled "Farm Cats," which gives excellent reasons for farmers to neuter their cat colonies. Go to www.cats.org.uk for ongoing news of this active organization, with its 263 branches, 28 shelters, and 8,000 volunteers—and its record of having helped to neuter more than 5 percent of all domestic cats in the United Kingdom.

221. *Newsletter 2000*, Celia Hammond Animal Trust, 6.

222. *Newsletter 2002*, Celia Hammond Animal Trust, 11.

223. Costa Blanca Feral Cat Trust website (www.feralcattrust.org.uk), downloaded 4 April 2003.

224. Jenny Remfry, letter to Ellen Perry Berkeley, 24 April 1999. This "heroic story," says Remfry, is recounted in detail in a book by Frank Wintle, *Helena Sanders and the Cats of Venice* (London: Souvenir Press, 1989).

225. Melissa Hart, "Gatti di Roma: The Torre Argentina Cat Sanctuary Welcomes Them All," *Cat Fancy* (April 2003), 40.

226. Celestine Bohlen, "A Slur, Cry Italy's Cat Ladies, and the Fur Flies," *New York Times*, 20 January 1995.

227. Lisa McDonald's history of her work with feral cats, 10 pages, sent to Ellen Perry Berkeley, 30 April 1999.

228. Ibid. McDonald was important to the cats in all these places—and more—encouraging people to do TNR, providing information from Alley Cat Allies, and often participating in the work herself.

229. Christine Pierson, letter to Ellen Perry Berkeley, 8 April 1999.

230. Christine Pierson, address to Animals Australia Conference (5 March 1999), 5.

231. Luis Varela, "Cubans Are Eating Cats," *The Bennington Banner* (Bennington, VT), 16 November 1994.

232. Statement by FOC (undated, 2 pages), 2; sent by Geoff Ingham to Ellen Perry Berkeley, 16 April 1999.

233. Lisa Clayton, "Feral Cats in Qatar," letter to the editor, *Best Friends*, a publication of Best Friends Animal Society (September/October 2003), 52.

234. Valery Garrett, "The Clipped Ear Club: Hong Kong Puts a Cap on Cats," *Animal Watch*, a publication of the American Society for the Prevention of Cruelty to Animals (Summer 2003), 54. Interestingly, as pointed out by Hong Kong resident Jill Robinson, founder of Animals Asia Foundation (speaking as part of the "Wildlife and Free-Roaming Cats" panel at the July 2003 Conference on Homeless Animal Management and Policy), TNR in Hong Kong is finding a lot of support from local residents, not only for TNR's humane considerations but also for its continued protection against the significant rat population of Hong Kong. It takes real work to tap this

support, of course. But real achievements are the product. Francis Battista of Best Friends Animal Society reported in *Best Friends* (November/December 2003), 27, that the HKSPCA had adapted "some of the best ideas from the West"—specifically, had "tapped into the grassroots world of feral cat caregivers, helping to develop more than 120 alley cat colony programs."

235. Emma Clifford (founder and project director, Animal Balance), speaking as part of the "Wildlife and Free-Roaming Cats" panel at the Conference on Homeless Animal Management and Policy, July 2003. A tape of this session can be obtained for $9.50, plus $3 shipping, from Professional Programs, P.O. Box 221466, Santa Clarita, CA 91322-1466; telephone: 661-255-7774. And visit www.animalbalance.org for ongoing reportage. *See also* Christine Rosenblat with Paul Glassner, "The San Francisco SPCA Is Making Waves Around the World," *Our Animals,* a publication of the SF/SPCA (Fall 2003), 30–31. The SF/SPCA is partnering with Animal Balance on this Galapagos effort, providing "personnel, equipment, supplies and advice," according to the *SF/SPCA eNews* of 8 May 2004, and is thereby helping to set up the same "M*A*S*H"-style clinics that have been so successful in the SF/SPCA's Feral Fix Program.

236. Rivi Mayer (founder and director) and Ellen Moshenberg, Cat Welfare Society of Israel, letters to Ellen Perry Berkeley, 3–16 December 2003. Visit the CWSI website (www.cats.org.il) for the full scope of this organization's activities. And think about the enormous progress already made in a place where a variety of negative attitudes—not unique to that place, certainly—must still be overcome for TNR to take hold completely. Ellen Moshenberg enumerates some of these attitudes: many people in Israel feel that spaying/neutering is "unnatural," many are "unwilling" (or unable) to spend money on an animal beyond feeding it, and many think that dumping is "perfectly acceptable." Considering the uphill battle that must be fought in every country where TNR is attempted, we can only marvel at the growing acceptance of TNR around the world. But think, too, about what Rivi Mayer says about TNR in Israel: with "lots and lots" of feral cat feeders, "it looked like TNR was just the idea they were waiting for!" (Lest we celebrate too soon, though, here is word from CWSI early in 2004: the Israeli Veterinary Services, fearing a spread of rabies from one rabid dog, began poisoning street cats and leaving them to die painful deaths in garbage bins. CWSI immediately joined this latest battle for a more up-to-date and less drastic response, winning an Israeli Supreme Court case against the killing of healthy street cats except when human health is expressly in danger. This judgment was a "clear victory" for TNR in "restricting the ability of

governmental authorities to do mass killing of cats," reports CWSI, and the cats got another "big win" when the court rejected an appeal.

237. Les Ward, Marchig Animal Welfare Trust, letter to Ellen Perry Berkeley, 29 March 2004.

238. Statement by FOC, op. cit., 2.

239. "The Feral Cat 'Problem' " (Friends of the Cat, undated, 4 pages), 2; sent by Geoff Ingham to Ellen Perry Berkeley, 16 April 1999.

240. D. W. Macdonald, N. Yamaguchi, and W. C. Passanisi, "The Health, Haematology and Blood Biochemistry of Free-Ranging Farm Cats in Relation to Social Status," *Animal Welfare*, a publication of Universities Federation for Animal Welfare, 7 (1998), 243–256.

241. Ibid., 254.

242. "HSUS Statement on Free-Roaming Cats," *Animal Sheltering*, a publication of The Humane Society of the United States (September-October 1998), 18.

243. Nathan J. Winograd, "Should We Rerelease FIV+ Cats?" a section of "Compassion Is the Way: The Care & Feeding of Feral Cats," a paper prepared for the "No More Homeless Pets" symposium sponsored by Best Friends Animal Sanctuary, now Best Friends Animal Society, 25–27 October 2002, Atlanta, GA, 10.

244. "Health Update: Overpopulation Kills More Cats Than Any Disease," *Alley Cat Action*, a publication of Alley Cat Allies (Winter 1999), 6. Even in a book published by Humane Society Press—*Community Approaches to Feral Cats: Problems, Alternatives & Recommendations*, by Margaret R. Slater—we see an alternative to the strict HSUS view. On p. 14, Slater writes this: "There is some debate about the need for FeLV and FIV testing, particularly if funds are scarce and such testing will mean that fewer cats will be sterilized as a result. One opinion is that cats in an area should be tested for a period of time to establish the prevalence of FeLV and FIV. Another opinion is that rates of infection typically are low in feral cat populations and that spaying and neutering, since they will decrease fighting, will also decrease transmission of the diseases."

245. "Call to Action: The Battle Over 'Alien & Exotic' Animals," *Alley Cat Action*, a publication of Alley Cat Allies (Fall 1999), 7. *See also* Isabelle M. Cote and William J. Sutherland, "The Effectiveness of Removing Predators to Protect Bird Population," *Conservation Biology* (April 1997). Interventions

can produce unexpected results indeed. Another example from the *Alley Cat Action* article: in trying to eradicate rats from New Zealand, because the rats were raiding birds' nests, a large rat population was poisoned. But then New Zealand's stoats, predators of rats, simply turned their attention to the endangered birds.

246. Charlie LeDuff, "Up, Down, In and Out in Beverly Hills: Rats," *New York Times* (17 September 2002).

247. Ibid.

248. Julie K. Levy, letter to Bradley J. Gruver (acting chief, Bureau of Wildlife Diversity Conservation, Florida Fish and Wildlife Conservation Commission), 6 May 2003.

249. Julie K. Levy, James E. Woods, Sherri L. Turick, and Donna L. Etheridge, "Number of Unowned Free-Roaming Cats in a College Community in the Southern United States and Characteristics of Community Residents Who Feed Them," *Journal of the American Veterinary Medical Association* 223:2 (15 July 2003), 202–205. This figure of 12 percent (combining the 14 percent among households that owned pets and the 10 percent among those that did not) is higher than other results cited in this paper, namely 10 percent of households feeding unowned cats in Santa Clara County, 9 percent of households in San Diego County, and 8 percent of households in Massachusetts. The compassionate people who are feeding feral cats can surely be a powerful force for the humane treatment of feral cats, but—as suggested by the researchers in this study of Alachua County—educational efforts for TNR should target more than just the pet owners, because a very large 45 percent of those feeding the free-roaming cats of Alachua County did not own pets.

250. Paul Leyhausen, letter to Ellen Perry Berkeley, 14 June 1982.

251. Lisa A. Centonze and Julie K. Levy, "Characteristics of Free-Roaming Cats and Their Caretakers," op. cit., 1630, 1633.

252. R. Lee Zasloff and Lynette A. Hart, "Attitudes and Care Practices of Cat Caretakers in Hawaii," op. cit., 242, 244.

253. Jenny Remfry, *Ruth Plant*, op. cit., 87–88.

254. Michael Mountain, "Playing God," *Best Friends*, a publication of Best Friends Animal Sanctuary, now Best Friends Animal Society (January/February 2001), 4.

255. Nathan J. Winograd, "Trap, Neuter, Return," a section of *Compassion Is the Way: The Care & Feeding of Feral Cats,"* op. cit., 4.

256. Nathan J. Winograd, "Should We Rerelease FIV+ Cats?" a section of *Compassion Is the Way: The Care & Feeding of Feral Cats,"* op. cit., 10. The question of whether cats live short and miserable lives is also excellently addressed by Winograd in his "Ferals, Ferals Everywhere, and Not Sure What to Do?" on No More Homeless Pets Forum, 8–12 September, 2003. Here, Winograd responds encouragingly to various questions from his experience as an attorney and a prosecutor; the 14-page text can be downloaded from www.bestfriends.org.

257. June Mirlocca (of Dedham, MA), *A Critical Evaluation of Free-Roaming /Unowned/Feral Cats in the United States: Proceedings of a Scientific Workshop Sponsored by the American Humane Association and the Cat Fanciers' Association,* op. cit., 70.

258. Jane C. Mahlow and Margaret R. Slater, "Current Issues in the Control of Stray and Feral Cats," *Journal of the American Veterinary Medical Association* 209:12 (15 December 1996), 2018.

259. "What Is a Feral Cat?" and "What Is TNR (Trap/Neuter/Return)?" on the Neighborhood Cats website (www.neighborhoodcats.org), downloaded 7 April 2003.

260. Cole McFarland, "Barn Cat Allies Forms from ACA Inspiration," *Alley Cat Action,* a publication of Alley Cat Allies, Summer 1993, 1, 4.

261. Roger Tabor, *Understanding Cats* (Devon: David & Charles, 1995; 1st United States edition, Reader's Digest Association, 1 May 1997), 144 pages.

262. "Wildlife Predation and TNR—Taking a Common Sense Approach," on the Neighborhood Cats website (www.neighborhoodcats.org), downloaded 1 December 2003. This is a point frequently made by Becky Robinson, national director of Alley Cat Allies, in her testimony before governmental commissions. In her letter of 6 May 2003, for instance, to Bradley J. Gruver, acting chief, Bureau of Wildlife Diversity Conservation, Florida Fish and Wildlife Conservation Commission, she notes strongly that the goal of those concerned with wildlife is the same as the goal of those carrying out TNR programs—i.e., to reduce the numbers of feral cats.

263. "SARS Kills Cat Program," *Animal People* (October 2003), 11. In a subsequent item about SARS, this publication reported the findings from a Rotterdam virologist suggesting that "cats raised for human consumption

may become a SARS vector—especially if the cats are caged at live markets near whatever as yet unidentified wildlife species is the primary SARS vector." (These findings, however, would seem to have more pertinence to the notorious live markets in Guangzhau, capital of Guangdong province in southern China, than to any well-managed feral cat colonies in TNR programs in Hong Kong, Singapore, etc.) *See* "Cat-Eaters May Get, Spread SARS," *Animal People* (November 2003), 11.

264. John W. Krebs, Heather R. Noll, Charles E. Rupprecht, and James E. Childs, "Rabies Surveillance in the United States During 2001" (with "2002 Rabies Update"), on the CDC website (www.cdc.gov/ncidod/dvrd/rabies), downloaded 11 November 2003. This paper also appeared in the *Journal of the American Veterinary Medical Association* 221:12 (15 December 2002), 1690–1701.

265. "Morbidity and Mortality Weekly Reports" on the CDC website (www.cdc.gov/ncidod/dvrd/rabies), downloaded 4 April 2003. All three of the human cases of rabies reported in 2002 (from California, Tennessee, and Iowa) were the result of bat bites. As the paper by Krebs, et al., makes clear, bats accounted for only 17.2 percent of all cases of animal rabies reported in 2001, but a bat bite—Krebs, et al., warn us—often goes unnoticed or is judged too insignificant to be of any consequence. This 17.2 percent for bats, as a percentage of all animal rabies in 2001, is to be compared with 37.2 percent for raccoons, 30.7 percent for skunks, 5.9 percent for foxes, 2.3 percent for all other wild animals, including rodents and lagomorphs, and—at 497 reported cases—6.7 percent for all domestic animals (including cats, dogs, cattle, horses, donkeys, mules, goats, and swine). Interestingly, Pennsylvania reported the largest number of rabid cats in 2001 (33 of the total 270 rabid cats across the United States). Nine other states reported more than 10 cases, while 19 states and the District of Columbia reported no rabid cats during 2001. We'd have to go back to 1975 to find a case of a cat transmitting rabies to a human, so there is certainly no justification for the scare-mongering that would link such transmissions—which haven't increased in a couple of decades—to TNR, which has increased vastly in these years.

266. As I wrote in my article "The Truth About Rabies," *I Love Cats* (March/April 1995), 24–27, relying on CDC statistics for the incidence of rabies in humans in the United States, and on World Health Organization estimates for the incidence of rabies in humans outside the United States, "Very few people get rabies in the U.S. today. It wasn't always so; during the late 1940s, an average of 40 people a year died a horrible death from rabies. With the

virtual elimination of canine rabies in the 1950s, the total dropped to an average of 11 people per year. From 1980 to 1994, no more than 3 people died a year in the U.S. of rabies; in several of these years, none. Comparing this with the 25,000 to 50,000 human deaths from rabies each year in India, we can appreciate the superb public health system we have in this country, and the excellent treatment available for anyone exposed to rabies." Current statistics for India put the number of cases of human rabies at only—only!—17,000 per year, according to the Asia for Animals conference held in September 2003 in Hong Kong. A report on this gathering appears in *Paws to Think*, a publication of The Pet Savers Foundation (Winter 2004), 13, 15. At this 2003 conference, it was further noted that the World Health Organization finds a dramatic decline in human rabies in the several cities in India where an effective Animal Birth Control program is in place. (This effort by Animal Birth Control, which neuters and vaccinates street dogs, was launched and is run by Blue Cross of India, an animal protection group.)

267. Merritt Clifton, "Where Cats Belong—and Where They Don't," op. cit., 17.

268. "'Managed' Cat Colonies: The Wrong Solution to a Tragic Problem," op. cit.

269. Daniel Castillo, "Population Estimates and Behavioral Analyses of Managed Cat (*Felis catus*) Colonies Located in Miami-Dade County, Florida, Parks," op. cit., iv.

270. "'Managed' Cat Colonies: The Wrong Solution to a Tragic Problem," op. cit., 3. This message, still on the website of the American Bird Conservancy, comes more than a decade after the "most common complaint"—about insufficient funds and caretakers for adequate management of TNR colonies—was noted in Passanisi and Macdonald's otherwise positive report. Since that time, great effort has been expended by many groups and individuals to provide funds, information, and encouragement to those doing TNR. There may be an occasional colony today that is not properly managed, but such an example can be considered rare. And even in the Passanisi and Macdonald report, done in 1990 for UFAW (a pioneer in the humane management of feral cats), this "most common complaint" was not sufficient to cause these two able researchers to condemn TNR.

Index

A

D

E

H

I

J

K

L

R

S

T

Ellen Perry Berkeley

An award-winning writer and editor, Ellen Perry Berkeley was the author of the first article on Trap-Neuter-Return (TNR) in an American publication (*Cat Fancy*, September 1984) and has since contributed regularly to the body of literature on feral cats in the United States. Her highly-acclaimed book, *Maverick Cats: Encounters with Feral Cats*, is a classic. First published by the New York publisher Walker & Company in 1982, it was reissued in paperback by New England Press in 1987. An expanded and updated edition came out in 2001 and the book was included on *Cat Fancy*'s list of "100 Great Moments for 20th Century Cats." Berkeley has written several other books and many articles on a variety of subjects following her time as a Senior Editor at the prominent professional journal the *Architectural Forum*. She has served on the Alley Cat Allies Board of Advisors since ACA was founded in 1990. With her husband Roy and their formerly feral cats, April, Leona, and Roscoe, Berkeley lives in Shaftsbury, Vermont, in a house of her own design.

PHOTO BY ROY BERKELEY